T0356699

··· THE ···
ARCHETYPE
EFFECT

· · · THE · · ·
ARCHETYPE
EFFECT

Unlocking the Six Types of
Motivation at Work

JAMES ROOT

WILEY

Published by John Wiley & Sons, Inc., Hoboken, New Jersey.
Published simultaneously in Canada.

For general information on our other products and services or for technical support, please contact our Customer Care Department within the United States at (800) 762-2974, outside the United States at (317) 572-3993 or fax (317) 572-4002.

Wiley also publishes its books in a variety of electronic formats. Some content that appears in print may not be available in electronic formats. For more information about Wiley products, visit our web site at www.wiley.com.

Library of Congress Cataloging-in-Publication Data

Names: Root, James (Writer of Archetype effect), author.
Title: The archetype effect : unlocking the six types of motivation at work / James Root.
Description: Hoboken, New Jersey : Wiley, [2025] | Includes index.
Identifiers: LCCN 2024037111 (print) | LCCN 2024037112 (ebook) | ISBN 9781394295210 (hardback) | ISBN 9781394295234 (adobe pdf) | ISBN 9781394295227 (epub)
Subjects: LCSH: Employee motivation. | Employee morale.
Classification: LCC HF5549.5.M63 R65 2025 (print) | LCC HF5549.5.M63 (ebook) | DDC 658.3/14—dc23/eng/20240917
LC record available at https://lccn.loc.gov/2024037111
LC ebook record available at https://lccn.loc.gov/2024037112

Cover Design: Jon Boylan
Cover Image: © Bain & Company
Author Photo: Courtesy of Rebecca Helene Hoffmann

SKY10095903_011025

For TSR and SJR, my greatest motivations

Contents

Contents

Prologue

Jing is having a bad week. She is 28 years old, a product manager at a young fintech business-to-business payments company in Shanghai. It was the role she was convinced she wanted from the time she joined the firm one year ago. Before the promotion and role switch into product management, she worked on policy and regulation. This week was hard because she's come to learn that her new role demands constant refereeing between the engineers and the go-to-market team, both of whom are noisy fanatics for their own points of view. Plus, one of the founders had shown up to a meeting unexpectedly (both founders had a habit of doing this), dominated the conversation for 10 minutes, confused everyone with new directions that implied delays to a planned release date, and then left the meeting without looking back. Jing's entire time as a product manager has been tough.

Growing up in a Tier 2 city in Zhejiang province, she was always a high-performing student. She could handle the 6.5-day school week and the 7:30 a.m. to 9 p.m. days, with the heavily programmed curriculum of math, Chinese, sciences, written English, geography, oral English, plus club activities like PE and music. Her father, who works for the local government, and her mother, a high school chemistry teacher, had sacrificed to get her into an academic (versus vocational) high school in their city and to hire the tutors required to keep her grades high. They vested many of their private hopes in Jing, an only child. Against almost impossible odds, making sacrifices of her own to study around the clock, she won a place at the nearest C9 college (equivalent to the Ivy League in the United States and the Russell Group in the United Kingdom) – Zhejiang University in Hangzhou.

She was recruited on graduation, along with a select few of her classmates, as an analyst in the e-commerce business of Alibaba. Alibaba's headquarters are in Hangzhou; the firm has close ties to the school. She found the "996" working norms (9 a.m. to 9 p.m., six days a week) to be demanding and exhausting, but she wanted to succeed. As someone who had always been at or near the top of her class at school and university, it was a shock when her first performance review said she was in the middle 60%, below the top 30%. Her parents worried too. She was less than three hours away from her home town, but hardly ever made it back for a visit.

She fought her way into the top 30% at her next performance review (although slipped back to the middle group in the following cycle), was promoted twice in the first three years, and received a special award for a team project that launched a new solution for the key opinion influencer program.

None of those achievements and recognitions gave her quite the sense of satisfaction and achievement she thought they would. Her whole life, it felt, she'd been driven to hit the next milestone, the next exam, to take the next win. Just over three years into a job at Alibaba that calibrated her performance against her peer group every six months, that demanded everything she could give in terms of hours and energy, she was starting to wonder if the role was right for her.

The most satisfaction she'd had recently was organizing a two-day customer event for dozens of big consumer brands to come in to Hangzhou, talk about their plans on the Alibaba platforms, and listen to a stream of Alibaba team members tell their stories about future improvements and opportunities. She wasn't in the spotlight, but behind the scenes she was the one making sure the production went smoothly and that all the speakers performed well.

She had also taken on a role as coordinator for onboarding the analysts (people like her, four years ago), which involved planning their training agenda, making sure they had mentors, and ensuring they were assigned to suitable projects in the first year. She thoroughly enjoyed this role and spent more time on it than she was notionally supposed to.

Suddenly, the unimaginable. She lost her job. In the face of a slowdown and competitive missteps, in the middle of COVID-19, Alibaba started a round of layoffs in 2022 that resulted in 20,000 people leaving the firm (another 20,000 were let go in 2023). Jing was devastated.

No matter how much her friends told her the layoff had nothing to do with her, the sense of failure and rejection was overwhelming. Worse than that, she felt failure and rejection about a job she was not even sure she was enjoying any more.

It took her a week to call home and break the news. Her father said she should focus on joining another prestigious company, with a good income and financial stability. Her mother said, "Look at me, I don't make a lot of money as a teacher, but I work so hard because I love to see my students doing well in my class and after they leave. Some of them come back years later to thank me."

Priority one for Jing was finding a new job. Alibaba had paid well, and with the help of her parents she had recently put down a deposit on an apartment. With her background and experience, the job search proved easier than she expected.

The payments firm was not prestigious in the way her father wanted; it was in Shanghai, farther from her home city; it did not pay as much as Alibaba; but they valued her skills in analytics, data management, and customer engagement, plus some experience working with engineering teams. They saw a path for her in product management, which for Jing and many like her, was considered a dream job. She thought that being a bigger fish in a small pond might be good for her career.

In her first few months at the new firm, she was back to the old Jing: motivated to deliver, working around the clock, proving to new colleagues that she could be trusted with the product manager promotion on the timeline they had agreed to.

Right on schedule, she was promoted. During her time in policy and regulation she had met a lot of people at the young firm but had not worked directly with the engineering teams. It was now clear to Jing that the tensions between the various groups, compounded by unpredictable founder interventions, were going to make her new role very challenging. She was not afraid of the hard work, and she still believed the product they were building was a good one, but she was starting to wonder why exactly she wanted the product manager job in the first place.

Introduction: The Mystery and the Moment

The Mystery

Why do you go to work? Who are you when you get there?

No, really. These are serious questions. How about the Gen Z marketer in the cubicle next to yours (if you still have a cubicle) – why does she go to work? Or the man in human resources who led your onboarding a couple of years ago? The engineer who drove your subway train this morning? The barista who made your coffee? The construction worker who built the office you are sitting in? The chief executive officer (CEO) of your firm, whom you have never met but seen on a few all-hands Zoom calls? What about the board director who voted to appoint that CEO?

Is it likely that each of these workers will have the same answers to these questions?

Not very likely. While there are important similarities in work motivation that cut across countries, job types, age groups, and genders, it turns out to be the differences that are most striking.

My colleagues at Bain and I have been talking to workers in 19 countries from all corners of the world, more than 48,000 of them so far – young, old; male, female; highly educated, much less educated; high, middle, and low income; care workers, service workers, manual workers, administrative workers, knowledge workers; workers in developed countries with aging workforces like Japan and Italy, workers in developing markets with young workforces like India and Nigeria. It is the largest and most global body of research on this topic that we know of.

Of course there are executives in the sample. They always attract attention. Far outnumbering the executives, we have listened to agricultural workers, construction and maintenance workers, customer service reps, food service workers, manufacturing workers, office administrative workers, resource extraction workers, retail salespeople, transportation workers, warehouse workers, architects, accountants, data analysts, engineers, finance professionals, information technology (IT) professionals, business consultants, marketing professionals, scientists, private security workers, legal professionals, graphic designers, academics, artists and entertainers, nurses and carers, doctors, journalists, law enforcement workers, librarians, workers serving in the military, psychologists, public officials, religious workers, social workers, teachers, travel guides . . . you get the idea. We made it a priority to hear from the full range of workers in all of the markets.

The main thing we observed is the rich diversity of motivations that bring people to work every day. Everyone has a personal algebra of motivation. Its roots may run deep, back to childhood, listening to your parents' dinner-time conversations about money and jobs; to school, the values it instilled and the skills it developed; to your early working experience, with a great boss or a horrible boss; to your current role. Or perhaps your motivation at work reflects some aspect of your intrinsic nature, however you choose to define that.

Six Worker Archetypes Emerge

Motivations might seem random at the individual level, but at scale, clear patterns emerge. The global research delivered something distinctly new. Six worker archetypes describe virtually all 48,000 individuals we surveyed. Two of them care mainly about relationships at work (*Givers* work to help others thrive; *Operators* like to have colleagues as friends but prefer to keep their heads down at work and take no risks).

Two of them care mainly about learning and growth (*Explorers* are highly motivated to try new things; *Artisans* want to achieve mastery of their domain).

The third pair care mainly about achievement at work (*Strivers* plan ahead and value the recognition of promotions; *Pioneers* want to change the world in some way and are comfortable taking risks to do so).

This insight about motivations arrives at a time of considerable complexity at work. There are talent shortages and talent mismatches in many firms. The workforce is shrinking in most developed economies and is on a similar path even in middle-income countries. And there are three trends, possible thanks only to technology, combining to change the relationship between individuals and firms.

Gig Work

First, gig work surged in prominence over the last 15 years, as platforms like Uber, DoorDash, Upwork, and their numerous global equivalents scaled up. We've seen this model before. Piecework has its origins in the guild system of medieval Western Europe and accelerated with the industrial revolution. In the late nineteenth century, the majority of factory workers earned piece rates: they were paid a fixed amount for each item made and were not employees of the firms they manufactured for. This model fell out of fashion as firms brought more and more activity in-house and worker rights improved during the twentieth century. By 2003, pre-smartphones, less than 5% of American workers were paid this way. Now, the idea is back, with a new name: the gig economy.

Today, there may be as many as 60M workers in the United States who are current or recent gig workers, being paid piece rates.[1] If that seems like a big number, consider China, where there are close to 200M gig workers, more than the entire working population of the United States and the United Kingdom combined.[2] This is not simply due to the rise of platform companies for ride-hailing and deliveries. It is also because the manufacturing base in China that used to offer full-time employment contracts to their assembly-line workers has shifted substantially to short-term contracts and more contingent work. There is a wide gap in job satisfaction between lower-income contract workers and their full-time counterparts doing exactly the same job. Ask the gig workers why, unsurprisingly, they cite income insecurity as one driver of lower satisfaction; the other is having little chance to make friends at work.

Flexible Work

Second, flexible work arrangements had been moving into the mainstream for several decades prior to the COVID-19 pandemic, when many of us found ourselves in a forced experiment about where and when work could get done.[3] It's hard now to find consensus among individuals or firms on the future model of working in the office/at home/somewhere else. The global workers we have studied are perfectly divided: one quarter would like to work from home all the time, one quarter never want to work from home again, and the remaining half are divided across one, two, three, and four days in the office.

Automation Anxiety

Third, automation anxiety is experiencing another spike, with the arrival of a new generation of artificial intelligence (AI) tools and applications. Firms are perpetually learning to do more with fewer people. The last 40 years of productivity gains have come from multiple sources: self-managing teams, the hollowing out of middle management, outsourcing, but above all, technology investment.

The anxiety is a long-running story. In *Modern Times* (1936), Charlie Chaplin's character is (unsuccessfully) fed his lunch by a machine as he tightens screws on an ever-accelerating assembly line. The message is clear: artisanal manufacturing jobs are being destroyed by rampaging automation. In the 1980s, with another wave of interest in AI and the increasing presence of personal computers, the zeitgeist's anxiety about job-killing machines appears in *Blade Runner* (1982) and *The Terminator* (1984). Soon after the launch of Apple's Siri, Spike Jonze's *her* (2013) presaged the twisting ambiguities in human relations with AI-powered virtual assistants.

These three tech-enabled disruptions have emerged at a moment in social history when many workers feel more able to be themselves at work. There are of course differences from country to country, and from work culture to work culture, but the days of toeing the line, of meekly accepting the bad assignment, of sucking it up, if not gone, are certainly in retreat. It's not perfect. Experts remind us that there is still plenty of "covering" at work, when employees are concerned about being judged, or discriminated against, for their unique identities, so they start to conceal or obscure their thoughts and opinions in an effort to fit in. But by comparison to a generation ago, let alone two, we have far more permission to be who we truly are at work.

The Myth of the Average Worker

The talent chessboard includes full-time employees, robots and AI of many kinds, contractors (often long term), gig workers, and employees of other firms in your ecosystem. The edges of the firm are becoming more porous. The ideas of a workplace and a worker are more fluid than they have been in 100 years. It's complicated.

Today, with these work disruptions and changes in social norms, one conclusion we can draw with confidence is that there is no longer such a thing as an *average* worker.

This begs the main question of this book – why should firms expect that having one way to do recruiting, one compensation model, one career path system, and one performance management system will allow all their people to bring their best selves to work?

The concept of *de-averaging* is nothing new. Customer segmentation has been mainstream business thinking for decades (there are even examples from the nineteenth and early twentieth centuries). The notion that buyers have distinct preferences that can be satisfied with distinct offerings and that they react to distinct messages is conventional. For just one example, the profitable growth and share gain of American Express from the early 1990s, after a period of stagnation, was built on a multiyear sequence of expansions from the original Green charge card to different spend tiers of charge card (Gold, Platinum) to credit cards to prepaid cards to co-branded credit cards with hotel chains and sports teams to cards for seniors and for students to cards with gift rewards and with cash rewards to corporate cards for purchasing departments and for small businesses – each new offering carefully designed for its distinct customer.

De-averaging has gone into overdrive in the last 20 years, with social media, search, location tracking, and online payments providing the fuel for acceleration. We take for granted how much Google or Amazon or Instagram or Tencent or Alibaba or Little Red or ByteDance or Flipkart or Grab or Careem or Naver or Kakao or Line know about us as consumers and shoppers. For the most part, while there are those who opt out, many of us seem happy to offer our personal information in return for more personalized communications and products.

The mystery is, why have we not applied this same thinking to our workers? Why do the firms who want to sell us their products, or sell our profiles to advertisers, know so much more about what motivates us than the firms we actually work for?

The prevailing ideas about the relationship between worker and firm were forged in a different world than today's, one where workers were viewed mostly as factors of production in the machine of enterprise. Today's firm requires a new mental model, one that humanizes the way we think about work and workers.

If we want all our workers to bring their best selves every day, we have to de-average them, not only on the basis of their skills but on their motivations. And from that understanding, build good jobs and career paths around what they want, not only what suits our systems best.

The Moment

This mystery, like all mysteries, must be seen in its context.

In sector after sector, insurgent firms are creating new ways to meet customer needs and trying to tilt the economic structure of an industry away from historic leaders.

Incumbent firms, with customer assets nurtured over decades, with systems and processes built for scale, can find it hard to be as fast and as responsive to customers as the younger firms with just a fraction of their history; but they are trying, many are succeeding, and more will.

The winning playbook is changing, which should come as no surprise. Looking back through the last several hundred years of business history, since global commerce began in earnest, the idea of the firm has evolved through a series of what we can now discern as definable eras: periods when particular strategies, corporate forms, financing sources, and styles of management are the dominant norm.

The primary trigger of a move from one era to another is the declining cost and increasing speed to move products, money, and information (for example, from horses to ships to railroads to airplanes; from mail to telegraphy to the Internet; from coins to checks to digital payments). Another trigger comes from the ratcheting expectations of consumers for more value and convenience. And there is always the genius of entrepreneur-leaders who find new solutions to the old problems and are willing to go to war with the status quo to serve customers better.

The New Era

Here in the mid-2020s, we are already in transition from one era of business to the next. Inevitably, winning strategies have to embrace new truths.

The Trade-Off Between Scale and Customer Intimacy Is Over

The first of these new truths is that the traditional trade-off between scale and customer intimacy is no longer a trade-off. Insurgents defy the sacred strategy text of the 1980s,[4] which laid down that your firm can either be low cost or be differentiated, but not both. How do they defy it? By being both. They see no problem with pursuing the benefits of massive scale (achieving low cost) at the same time as delivering previously unimaginable degrees of customer intimacy (being differentiated). Even the newly termed *hyperscalers* should really be called the *hyperscaler-hyperintimates*, because all of them are both.

Algorithms like Amazon Recommendations or Netflix Suggestions typify the booming capability to offer the benefits of scale (the low cost of Amazon's procurement, warehousing, and distribution network; Netflix's investment in content) combined with extremely high degrees of personalization or customer intimacy. Starbucks offers an intimate relationship with your barista, who knows your name and your daily order, plus the scale-driven benefits of the loyalty program and the mobile ordering app. We are a long way from Henry Ford pursuing the scale benefits of continuous assembly for the Model T by eliminating customer choice completely ("any color, so long as it's black").

New Ways to Manage Workers

The second new truth is about us, the workers.

More work is being automated. More work is being outsourced to ecosystem partners. More firms are testing new methods of working, often with self-managing teams setting their own objectives. More firms want to push decision-making and accountabilities down to the front line, where the

Introduction: The Mystery and the Moment

organization meets the customer. There is more use of gig workers and contractors to manage capacity and for specialized expertise, more cross-functional teaming, more peer-to-peer information flow, more continuous feedback rather than once-a-year top-down performance evaluations, more team-based incentives.

With more automation, more outsourcing, and more self-managing teams, head count at the typical firm will fall, all other things equal. Just as measures of plant asset efficiency became less meaningful in a world of outsourced manufacturing, traditional measures of overhead efficiency are losing relevance in the era of scale insurgency. Long-held ideas about appropriate spans and layers are being challenged. In the parts of the business using self-managing teams, for instance, the proper span might not be the usual 6 to 8, but 20, or why not 30?

The role of the generalist professional manager, enshrined at the center of almost all large organizations for the last 100 years, is diminishing, not to nothing, but at least relegated in comparison to the mission-critical roles – those roles that truly deliver the firm's promise to its customers.

Winning insurgents do not organize around professional managers or use spans and layers as their default technique to handle growth. Insurgents value individual contributors just as highly as managers, and some (e.g. Tencent[5] and Shopify,[6] two of numerous examples) organize career paths around the choice to become a manager or not.

Jensen Huang, founder and CEO of NVIDIA, the platform computing firm powering much of the current AI advance, has somewhere between 50 and 60 direct reports.[7] His logic is that CEOs can have a large number of reports because the people who report to a CEO require the least amount of oversight, leaving CEOs with more bandwidth than other managers. This is a

Introduction: The Mystery and the Moment

very different way of leading than the traditional "6 to 12" direct CEO reports that became the norm 30 years ago.

We have moved on. We are well advanced into the first phase of the era of scale insurgency. With that move, the norms of talent management are going to change.

This is the moment, and as it meets the mystery, we are seeing an explosion of experiments in people management.

The experiments still have a long way to go before we settle on a set of new norms. The playbook is always being tinkered with and adjusted for special situations. This can be exciting for those in the labs designing the experiments and for the subjects, all of us who work. In one regard, though, the designers in the human resources (HR) labs have gone too far and need to reset.

It is now the conventional wisdom in some parts of the world that what matters above all else is for humans to find their meaning and purpose in their work.

Our research tells a different story. The search for individual meaning and purpose through work, or at work, is very important . . . *but only to some workers.* An extreme version of this search is described in Professor Carolyn Chen's 2022 book *Work Pray Code.*[8] Chen explores how Silicon Valley tech companies bring religion into the workplace, replacing traditional forms of worship, blurring the line between work and religion, and transforming the nature of spiritual experience in modern life.

The workers she studies, many of whom are engineers, entrepreneurs, and founders at tech firms, exhibit behaviors associated with religious devotion, such as long hours, zealous commitment to their work, and a sense of mission or calling. Work satisfies their needs for belonging, identity, purpose, and transcendence that religion once met. This must be sensationally satisfying for them.

It is true that in some developed, Western societies including the United States, there is a well-documented retreat from organized religion and from the joining of groups and clubs that historically promoted trust and community cohesion. There is a rise in loneliness and isolation. A vacuum has appeared in some people's lives that work could step in to fill.

But we should not make sweeping, averaged-out assumptions about why people go to work and what they are looking for when they get there. Their answers vary so much. For many, it is to provide for the needs of themselves and their family. For others, it's to be with friends and enjoy camaraderie. For others, it's about learning and exploring through work. For others, it's about pursuing milestones and being recognized. None of these motivations should be considered somehow "higher" or "lower" in a hierarchy than the others – they are simply the ones that mean most to that worker at that time in their life. We risk allowing what may be a *WEIRD* (Western Educated Industrial Rich Democratic) perspective about meaning and purpose at work to obscure the reality for the great majority of workers.

Even if we stay in the United States and pull back the camera a little from the intensely narrow confines of Silicon Valley, we will find Beverley, a 45-year-old senior manager at a telecommunications company, who puts it this way: "Honestly, my job is just a job. My meaning and purpose come after I'm done with my work."

We do a grave disservice to Beverley, and the millions of others like her, and we commit a serious mistake in talent management if we conclude that she just has not found her meaning and purpose at work yet, so we must create more ways to nudge her toward it.

To be clear, I am greatly enthused by the search for personal meaning and purpose at work . . . *for those workers who care*. Some people who search for meaning and purpose in life will look for it outside work, some at work. All these types of worker exist and sit alongside us every day. It is important in the new norms to rewrite the popular (but unsupported) assumption that finding meaning and purpose in work is the ultimate point of arrival for everyone and that those of us who do not are less effective, less productive, and less valuable.

I am also greatly enthused when *firms* develop for themselves a statement of purpose – a mission or vision. I have worked with multiple firms to support them doing precisely this and have seen the powerful integration that a well-considered corporate purpose or mission can bring. There are those for whom a firm's mission is very important as they make career decisions. It varies from country to country but averages out to just over 30% of all workers. They tend to be more satisfied at work than others for whom a firm mission is not important. But this is not the same as expecting individuals to find personal meaning and purpose at work in order to perform well, feel satisfied, and contribute differentially. Many high performers look for no such thing. Let us not assume that worker motivations are more or less all the same, because they aren't.

De-averaged, Re-humanized, Good Jobs

It is time to apply the same tools we have long used with customers to our own workers. Winning firms of the future do this and point the way to a world of work where more good jobs are created and matched to the right individuals.

In the old talent model there were "managers" and "labor." The underlying assumption was that each employee was a unit, with its own experience and ability, moving through the system to become a better worker, or a better manager, or sometimes to migrate from laboring to managing. Everyone was trying to improve whatever it was they did, with a goal of rising through the organization. Individual motivations barely mattered at all. This assumption was so pervasive that every aspect of the standard organization model was built around it. Rewards, reporting structures, decision rights, performance reviews – all the elements lined up.

When we explore the archetypes in detail, you will see that there was an unexamined belief baked in to the old norms that most people are *Strivers* at work. Many of the standard talent management systems are built for Strivers – this is part of the reason they are all so alike from one firm to the next.

What's now becoming clear is that some highly effective organization models, including those developed by scale insurgents, do not require every worker to try to advance up the hierarchy. There are plenty of roles where personal progress, results, and success are defined differently.

Also now clear is that it was a myth all along to assume every worker wanted the same path. As you will see, what people want in a job, and who they are at work, is richly varied. A talent system that knows what each wants, what each is stressed by, and what gives each energy can create good jobs for all types of worker – good jobs for the individual and good jobs for their firm.

The six worker archetypes can replace this rudimentary manager/labor taxonomy. Each has its own path to full potential at work, while sharing some common values and behaviors. Understanding archetypes can help all of us be more effective working on diverse teams in diverse organizations. It can help us unlock the potential at the edges of our firm, with older workers, and younger workers. It can help to head off the conflicts between leaders and those they lead that are based in their different motivations. Understanding archetypes helps us create good jobs, where worker satisfaction and business results converge.

How to Read This Book

This book is for you if you want a new way to understand what motivates you at work every day and why you feel how you feel when you get there. It aims to give you a language for talking with your firm about your current role, your future choices, and your career options. If you have already answered those questions in full, true congratulations: please help the rest of us by sharing your story with colleagues and friends. Gen Z marketers, train engineers, baristas, construction workers, CEOs, board directors – any of us may feel we are in roles that somehow do not fully suit us or that we have had to make too many adjustments in ourselves to meet our firm's expectations about the behaviors and values appropriate for that job. Any of us may equally feel that sense of flow that shows up when we have a good job, which feels like an extension of what we have always wanted to do, with challenges, recognition, relationships, rewards, trust, opportunities to grow, all in just the right proportions for us.

The way to understand the feelings that I describe in this book is not as an abstract psychological riddle, like some other typing frameworks. These archetypes emerged first from listening to tens of thousands of people around the world talk about their jobs, what they value, what they like, what stresses them out, how they deal with the grind, what their fears about work are, how they find confidence in their ability to do a good job; and then from applying common sense to the highlights of those conversations to make them actionable.

This book is also for you if you are a leader frustrated by the lack of change in your firm's talent systems. You want the same from your people management teams as you do from your product, sales, and marketing teams: different solutions for different profiles and preferences. What follows describes a way to accelerate progress.

In Chapter 1, I tackle the origins of the talent management assumptions and systems that we still see in use today. I retell the story of Frederick Taylor and his Scientific Management method in a way that puts the human worker at the center of his studies. I then look at some of the talent experiments of more recent times.

Chapter 2 describes the six worker archetypes that have emerged from our research. I hope you recognize yourself in one (or maybe more) of the six.

Chapter 3 describes some case studies and observations about putting archetypes into action.

Chapter 4 discusses leaders. They think about the same factors that all workers consider, putting their own weightings on particular values and job attributes and using their own models of decision-making. Two stories – one about Alfred Sloan of General Motors, one about a fourteenth-century Italian entrepreneur – illustrate different archetypes in leadership roles.

In Chapter 5, I talk about energy, stress, and wellness at work. This is a topic of current interest in many workplaces. I try to link general observations with what matters for each archetype.

In Chapter 6, I highlight some of the important differences for older, younger, female and male workers. It is important to understand these differences if we are going to build successful, diverse, multigenerational workplaces.

Chapter 7 concludes the book with more discussion of good jobs. Encouraging firms to build good jobs rooted in the skills they need *and* the motivation of each archetype is the ultimate objective of this book. What are good jobs, and how can we get better at creating them?

One more thing. You will enjoy this book more if you know your own archetype. Go to https://www.bain.com/insights/six-worker-archetypes-for-the-world-ahead-future-of-work-report-interactive and answer the quick quiz. It takes just a minute.

By the way, I am a Striver. There is a lot of Giver in me too, it turns out. I had to become an older worker to understand that.

Chapter 1

Old Norms, New Norms

In 1930, John Maynard Keynes predicted that continued eco-nomic growth over the course of the twentieth century would reduce the workweek to 15 hours.[1] In 1959, the US Postmaster General predicted that today's mail would be sent by rockets (email turned out to be more cost-effective, faster, and, I think, more environmentally sustainable).[2] In 1964, the RAND Corporation predicted that by 2020 we would be breeding intelligent apes to perform manual labor.[3]

We are not very good at forecasting the future of work. Perhaps it's no surprise that Keynes imagined a gradual disappearance of work, given what was happening in the decades prior to his prediction. Between 1870 and 1930, the average weekly hours of a nonagricultural worker in the United States fell by one quarter, from 59.5 hours to 44.5.

This downward trend continued, if more slowly, in the second half of the twentieth century. One study of time use in the United Kingdom found that between 1961 and 2000, average weekly leisure time increased by seven hours for men and five hours for women.[4]

Only one group of workers bucked this trend. Top quintile earners – for whom busyness became a symbol of status and success – saw their average weekly hours creep up, from 39.7 in 1973 to 42 in 2018. They now work the longest hours of all: the idle rich of bygone days has become the laboring class of today. Those at the bottom of the income hierarchy work the least hours, unable often to secure the stable full-time employment they need and want.

The importance we place on our jobs compared with other life factors has declined across successive generations. According to the World Values Survey, younger generations place a lower importance on work relative to leisure time compared with earlier generations who took the survey at the same age. The only outlier is Gen X – hit particularly hard in wealth and career prospects by the 2008–2009 financial crisis.

On average, as countries grow their per capita gross domestic product (GDP), workers gain greater economic freedom to spend time on other pursuits. This trend is not confined to the West: workers in China and India are also starting to place less importance on work relative to leisure.

Was Keynes simply too early with his prediction? Maybe not. As of 2017, only 28% of Americans said they would stop working altogether if they had enough money for the rest of their lives – down a little from 34% in 1995.[5]

The predictions keep coming. In late 2023, the much-quoted Elon Musk said of AI that "We will have something that is, for the first time, smarter than the smartest human. It's hard to say exactly what that moment is, but there will come a point where no job is needed. You can have a job if you want one for personal satisfaction. But AI will do everything."[6]

So, there's that. If Musk is right and "that moment" is within planning distance, then this book, with its focus on humans at work, is far too narrowly defined. For now, I shall assume, while allowing for the possibility Musk means what he says, that we are a very long way from a human-free workforce.

The Professional Management System

In 1961 the General Motors Personnel Staff published *The Secret of Getting Ahead*.[7] Here is the opening of the pamphlet, with its startlingly simple message for the men and women of GM:

> WOULD YOU LIKE TO GET AHEAD in this world? Then learn how to please your boss. It is the only way you can possibly succeed at anything. The sooner you recognize it, the faster your progress will be. Do you find this idea unpleasant? Millions of people do. Yet all their combined resentment cannot change the situation one iota. It's one of the facts of life. The people who do not adjust to it never get anywhere. The promotions and pay raises which might have been theirs go to someone else.
>
> I mentioned this fact recently to my nephew, Jim, who is just finishing college. If he wanted to get ahead, I pointed out, he would have to learn to please his boss. Jim bristled. It was as if I had suggested that he demean himself and lower his personal standards. Jim's reaction was perfectly normal. I can remember feeling the same way myself. Young people have a natural resentment of bosses; they do not like the idea of having to please any specific individual. They feel, somehow or other, that there ought to be certain standards of conduct or performance. If you reach or exceed those standards your success ought to be assured. It should not be a matter of anyone's opinion.
>
> But who is going to set these standards? And who is going to judge whether or not they have been fulfilled? No matter how you look at it, the first requirement of

Old Norms, New Norms

any job is that a man be helpful to his boss. That's why he was hired – to help his boss carry out the duties for which his boss is responsible. And who is in a better position to judge whether he has done this successfully than the boss himself?[8]

OK, Boomer. Try that in next month's Town Hall meeting. My point is neither to criticize nor make fun of General Motors. In fact, I would make a strong case that Alfred Pritchard Sloan, Jr. – a leader at GM from 1916 when his company was acquired and later president and then CEO of the whole group – was the most impactful, most important businessperson of the twentieth century. He is the leader, more than any other, who shaped the norms of professional management, and I talk about him in more detail in Chapter 4.

The Birth of Professional Management

It is easy to forget why professional management took off. The previous era (in the United States) had been dominated by trusts – big, powerful, founder-led companies that were vertically and horizontally integrated to a degree that would make today's tech hyperscalers blush. The likes of Standard Oil, US Steel, and the American Tobacco Company all thrived, until a wave of antitrust regulation and rapid technological change left them vulnerable to a new breed of highly efficient competitor.

The professionalization of management enabled a new generation of companies to scale and sustain themselves beyond the vision of a charismatic founder. Smart managers, trained in the latest techniques, made data-driven choices about strategy (where to play and how to win). They built systems for continuous improvement and to enable better, fairer, and more consistent decision-making. They increased transparency and managed risk.

Standardization, routines, predictability – this is what professional management delivers. The benefits are evident: the cost advantages of scale, the easy spread of learning across the firm, and the eventual market power and influence.

Consider the shipping container.[9] It standardized an industry and created a routine to dramatically lower the cost of ocean freight. The first standard shipping container was invented and patented by Malcolm McLean in 1956. He wasn't a shipper. In fact, he owned the largest trucking company in the United States at the time.

For years, as McLean was building his trucking company, sea-borne cargo was loaded and unloaded in odd-sized wooden cases. He watched dock workers unloading freight from trucks and transferring it to ships and was perplexed by the inefficiency. He knew that both trucking carriers and shipping companies would gain from a standardized process of cargo transfer. He slowly developed the idea to make intermodal transportation seamless and efficient.

To start the change, he acquired the Pan Atlantic Tanker Company, with all its shipping assets. He started experimenting to find better ways to load and unload his trucks.

Eventually, he developed what we now call a shipping container. It is strong, theft resistant, reliable, and easy to transfer. In April 1956, the first container shipped, departing from Port Newark, successfully plying its route to Houston.

Standard containers have changed international trade. Cargo now goes on its journey sealed and safe, which reduces pilfering and damage. Containers have reduced the labor required for loading and unloading and have changed the character of port cities worldwide. Cranes substituted for human labor;

ports evolved to accommodate larger ships and loading facilities. McLean's innovation reduced the expense of international trade and increased its speed by shortening shipping time. This is a quintessential professional management–era achievement.

General Electric's famous leadership training center at Crotonville in New York state trained generations of leaders in playbooks for strategic planning, Six Sigma, lean manufacturing, just-in-time, and Net Promoter System, among other tools. The GE managers could disperse back to their jobs equipped with a common language and shared techniques for managing the diverse businesses. (The center was closed in 2022 as part of a broader set of changes at the, by then, much-diminished GE.)[10]

The professional management system has been written off many times but has endured the rise of the shareholder-value movement in the 1970s, deregulation in the 1980s, globalization in the 1990s, multiple technology boom-and-bust cycles, and a global financial crisis. It soldiered on through a worldwide epidemic and during that time showed some of its greatest strengths.

Alfred Sloan wrote a book after he had retired from the CEO role at General Motors, published in 1963. It is called, with scant regard for the marketing campaign, *My Years with General Motors*, and is just that: a sober, factual, mostly chronological account of his 46 years with the firm.[11]

By that time, the same time as the personnel staff were preparing *The Secret of Getting Ahead*, GM was the largest private industrial enterprise on Earth, with more than 1M shareholders, 600,000 employers, more than $9B in assets, close to $15B in sales, and $1.5B in profits. For another perspective on how big the firm was, the 1962 GM would be on the 2023 Fortune 500 list, somewhere around #55 by inflation-adjusted revenue (the actual 2023 GM was ranked #25).

My Years with General Motors tells the story of the changes to the organization that Sloan put in place to respond to the challenges and opportunities that came with all the growth. We hear of the ebbs and flows between divisions (who owned the car brands and the consumer relationships); staff groups such as finance; and general officers (including Sloan himself). Activity by activity – from Procurement to Advertising to Technical Engineering to Sales – Sloan describes the meticulous design of committee structures, most of which he did himself, to manage the three different groups involved in these functions.

Sloan also had a prophetic grasp of customer segmentation. His desire to be the "anti-Ford" in the emerging automotive industry led to the idea that GM would make six car models, with the price and features of each model conceived in relation to the entire range.

The advertising slogan he adopted to promote this approach was "a car for every purse and purpose." I have in front of me a 1925 print ad for GM with that exact headline, which says "General Motors offers 46 types of open and closed cars ranging in price from $525 to $4,485" and then, somewhat laboriously, goes on to list them.

Sloan understood his customers had all sorts of motivations for buying a GM car. He also understood the different activities of his firm required people with highly distinct skills and styles. I believe his thinking about people at work was influenced by the work of Frederick Winslow Taylor.

Scientific Management

Frederick Winslow Taylor had a nickname. He was known as Speedy. I always assumed this reflected his obsession with efficiency, which was his life's work and the subject of his book,

The Principles of Scientific Management, published in 1911, just a few years before he died at the age of 59.[12]

But there might have been other reasons for the nickname. Taylor was an athlete of the highest order. He was a US national tennis player and won the doubles at the inaugural US National Tennis Championships – precursor to what is now the US Open – at Newport, Rhode Island, in 1881. As if that were not enough, at the 1900 Summer Olympics, in Paris, he came in fourth ... but not in tennis – in golf, behind an American and two Scots. This suggests some prodigious talent.

Speedy on the court and on the fairway too, perhaps.

Taylor had one big idea about work, and he spent his life designing it, perfecting it, implementing it at the firms where he worked, and later selling his expertise as an adviser to other firms looking for similar results. He also made his fortune relatively early on in life – in his 40s – *and* he had been born into a prosperous, professional family.

We generally refer to Taylor's idea as *scientific management*, a term he did not invent but was happy to embrace. *The Principles of Scientific Management* is a crisp, 76-page essay, with its objectives clearly laid out up front. He says he wants to:

- Point out the great loss in the country from inefficiency
- Convince the reader that the solution is systematic management rather than searching for a "great man"
- Prove that the best management is a science, based on laws, rules, and principles

His motivation is maximum prosperity for the employer *and* for each employee. Scientific management, he says, is an alignment of the interests on both sides: workers want higher wages, and employers want lower labor costs. They can both get what they want if they understand that maximum prosperity is achieved when the individual reaches maximum efficiency.

This equation, that maximum prosperity requires maximum efficiency, is so self-evident to Taylor, he gets agitated at the idea that anyone could fail to understand it. Apparently unaware of the old adage that you lose half your audience the moment you talk about sport, he reached for a metaphor: "The English and American people are the greatest sportsmen in the world. Whenever an American workman plays baseball, or an English workman plays cricket, it is safe to say that he strains every nerve to secure victory for his side [...] any man who fails to give out all there is in him in sports is branded as a quitter, and treated with contempt by those who are around him."[13]

It is safe to say that sentence has not aged well, but it is setting up a line of thought vital to Taylor. He assumes that "when that same workman returns to work on the following day" (he means the day after giving his all representing his nation in an epic contest of run-scoring), "this man deliberately plans to do as little as he safely can, to turn out far less work than he is well able to."[14]

This conscious underperformance Taylor calls "soldiering," and it offends him. (Soldiering foreshadows "quiet quitting" and "lying flat," which offend some commentators today.) He does not simply blame the workers. He also blames the managers for allowing poor relationships between employer and employee to exist and for failing to have a data-driven way to know what the right rate of production actually is.

We're deep into a Dilbert universe here, where the boss knows nothing and everyone else is trying to minimize effort and avoid accountability. As Taylor saw it, the worker's natural laziness and systematic soldiering combine to reduce prosperity for all.

Taylor was well educated; he attended Phillips Exeter Academy in the 1870s and was lining up to study law at Harvard. He'd already passed the entrance exams with honors when he decided to pursue a different path.

He apprenticed as a machinist and eventually joined the Midvale Steel Company machine shop in 1878. At the age of 22, he started as a day laborer because there were no full-time positions open when he applied. When the clerk of the shop was fired, Taylor stepped into that role.

In time, he was promoted to machinist, running a lathe. Then to gang-boss of all the lathe operators. Then to foreman of the machine shop. And eventually to chief engineer of the entire works. All told, he spent more than 25 years at the front line of heavy manufacturing.

He had traveled in Europe as a young man, but when it came to his career, he stayed more or less completely put in the Northeastern United States, mostly in and around Pennsylvania, the state of his birth. Midvale was located outside Philadelphia, and when he moved on from there, it was first to the Manufacturing Investment Company of Philadelphia, which owned paper mills, and then later, in 1898, to Bethlehem Steel, also in Pennsylvania, where he was specifically hired to help them solve a machine shop capacity problem.

It was while at Bethlehem Steel, together with his colleague Maunsel White, that Taylor developed a process for treating high-speed tools with tungsten, which enabled them to double or even triple their cutting speeds. The Taylor-White process was patented and made Taylor a wealthy man, which in turn enabled him to spend the rest of his life exploring and expanding his theory of scientific management, consulting and writing and giving talks.

Those early years at Midvale will have afforded Taylor the opportunity to observe workers and management at close range. What he saw was that the same job was being done by different people in totally different ways. Because nothing was written down, management was completely at the mercy of the *initiative* of the worker when it came to executing the task. And in his view the employees will never give the employer their full initiative because they believe that would be against their best interests.

Therefore, the employer has to offer some special *incentive* to the workers – maybe higher wages or the hope of faster promotion or shorter hours or better working conditions – whatever might get the employee to deliver what was actually possible.

These two ideas, *initiative* and *incentive*, formed the basis of what Taylor calls, dismissively, *ordinary management*. Workers give their best initiative only when a special incentive is in place.

For Taylor, this was ridiculous. Under scientific management, much higher efficiency will be achieved, for two reasons. First, managers will gather all the knowledge possessed by the workers about each task, classify it, tabulate it, and produce rules, formulae, and laws so the *initiative* of each worker will be exactly the same, because everyone will know what is actually possible in terms of output.

Second, management will take on new roles: they will replace rule-of-thumb practices with science, they will select the best workers and train them, and they will cooperate with the workers to make sure that scientific management principles are being used. Overall, there will be a more even split of tasks between workers and management.

Pig Iron and Schmidt

Much of his book is taken up with stories about real-life experiments in scientific management. The first and most famous one is about pig iron handling in the Bethlehem Steel plant.

In case you are a little rusty on the steel manufacturing processes, pig iron, also known as *crude iron*, is an intermediate product in the manufacture of steel, which you get by smelting iron ore in a blast furnace.

The traditional shape of the molds used for pig iron ingots is a branch structure with the individual ingots at right angles to a central channel, so it sort of resembles a litter of piglets being nursed by a sow.

At the Bethlehem Steel plant, the average man loaded 12.5 tons of pig iron a day. Taylor and his people did their first "time and motion" study and concluded that the real number should be 47 tons per day. They had studied 75 workers in the plant, picked 4 of them as being of the right stuff, and then narrowed down to one he calls "Schmidt" as his test case.

There has been speculation about Schmidt. Did he actually exist? Is he a composite? Did Taylor fake Schmidt's output numbers to goose his productivity targets in the study? We will never know, but Schmidt did give Taylor a rare opportunity for some humor, as he replicated Schmidt's accent in print. I do not know if Taylor was a funny man. In the book, he comes across as mostly brusque and humorless, but when it comes to Schmidt, he really lets go.

This is literally as he writes it in the book, a conversation between himself and Schmidt:

> "Schmidt, are you a high-priced man?"
> "Vell, I don't know vat you mean."
> "What I want to find out is whether you are high-priced man or one of those cheap fellows? What I want to find out is whether you want to earn $1.85 a day or whether you are satisfied with $1.15?"
> "Did I vant $1.85 a day? Vas dot a high-priced man? Vell, yes, I was a high-priced man."[15]

My assumption is that Schmidt was German; Hungarian is also possible.

After all the measuring and refining and training, Schmidt increases his output to 47.5 tons a day, his wages go up 60% as a result, and eventually they train all the workers to shift pig iron at this new, much higher rate, using the principles of scientific management.

After pig iron, Taylor moves on to a lengthy experiment with shovels, to illustrate that the use of implements is a crucial factor in productivity, too. The shovels story also introduces one innovation that is strikingly modern.

Every morning, each worker received two pieces of paper in his pigeonhole. The first told him which implements to get from the tool room and where to start work that day. The second told him the history of his prior day's work, including how much money he had made. With this one new behavior, each worker was suddenly an individual, not merely a gang member.

This is something critics miss about Taylor. He *is* an advocate for the individual at a time when in manufacturing – just as in agriculture – the workers were generally considered as fungible resources, parts of "crews" or "gangs." Toward the end of the essay, he says this: "…the time is coming when all great things will be done by that type of cooperation in which each man preserves his own individuality and is supreme in his particular function, and each man at the same time loses none of his originality and proper personal initiative, and yet is controlled by and must work harmoniously with many other men."[16]

With updated language and looser grammar, this would nicely describe ways of working at Spotify, and any firm where the role of individual contributors is highly valued.

Later he describes in detail his work in a factory making bicycle balls, which is to say the polished steel balls used in bicycle bearings – a product whose final inspection was critical to quality control.

One hundred and twenty women were enrolled in the test, the most experienced testers of ball bearings in the plant. Taylor gradually reduced their working hours, from 10.5 a day to 10, then 9.5, then 9, and finally 8.5, keeping their pay the same and observing that output increased each time the hours were reduced. He introduced the "differential rate piecework," by which the pay for each woman was increased in proportion to the quantity of her output but also (and still more) in proportion to the accuracy of her work. By the end of the test, the accuracy of the work at the higher speed was two-thirds greater than at the former, slower speed.

In all these stories, Taylor's system for improvement is largely physical. First, through trial and error, establish the very best movements by which a task should be completed. Then, do the same for the tools. Then, train everyone in the new movements.

Scientific management recognized the importance of motives. Taylor believed a worker needed a daily task, not just an instruction to "do as much as you can." And he believed that bonuses for exceeding the task should be very substantial. He also understood that change takes time. He said that management should assume two to three years (sometimes as long as five) to change worker behavior.

One modern executive who might appreciate aspects of scientific management is Jeff Bezos, executive chair of Amazon. This comes from his 2020 shareholder letter:

> "We don't set unreasonable performance goals. We set achievable performance goals that take into account tenure and actual employee performance data. Performance is evaluated over a long period of time as we know that a variety of things can impact performance in any given week, day, or hour."[17]

That framing could be Exhibit A for the pro-Taylorists. Their view is that he deserves to be thought of alongside Ford and Edison as one of the absolute greats of business. His theories may not be much discussed today because we *all* live in his world of time and motion, performance metrics, best practices, systems, and processes. Taylorism is everywhere in business, in government, in the military, and in nonprofits. It's everywhere in life. It's so deeply embedded you cannot even see it.

There is an alternative reaction, though: the negative view of Taylorism. Scientific management is dehumanizing. It oppressively subordinates workers to management, leading to worker alienation. Its obsession with efficiency ignores other benefits that are harder to measure, like social values. Most biting of all – and this was a criticism leveled at Taylor in particular by post-war Japanese business thinkers – it's not even a sensible approach, because it assumes that workers are stupid and only managers (who do not actually do the work) have the ability to drive continuous improvement.

Taylor's approach does work at some very fundamental level. Eliminating variability in a process through systematic and continuous improvement will drive down costs per unit to their lowest level. Sharing learning from one worker to the next or from one shift to the next or from one plant to the next will invariably help to push operating costs down and productivity up.

But his assertion that scientific management is an aligning of the interests of management and workers is disingenuous. In the shovels experiment, the results were so impressive that the size of the workforce was reduced from around 400 to 140. By the end of the ball bearings productivity improvements, 35 women were doing the work that previously required 150. This is hardly maximizing prosperity for everyone. He acknowledges this in a roundabout way, with the slippery logic that not everyone is suited to all tasks.

This is *the* jobs debate of our time – what robots and automation tools and generative AI do is take Taylorist principles to tasks that can be redesigned to eliminate human involvement.

The Hawthorne Experiments

Another important input to the jobs debate emerged in the decade after Taylor's death, when the National Research Council began to conduct experiments at the Hawthorne Works, a Western Electric facility in Cicero, a suburb of Chicago in Illinois. Western Electric was the sole supplier of telephone equipment to AT&T in the 1920s, and Hawthorne was its most sophisticated plant.

What would a modern equivalent be? Something akin to launching productivity research today at the Longhua plant of Foxconn in Shenzhen, where several hundred thousand workers (and a lot of robots) assemble Apple iPhones. Or perhaps at TSMC's main center for semiconductor fabrication in Hsinchu Science Park in Taiwan. Put another way, Hawthorne was not a place where pig iron was being hefted around by Schmidt: it was a place of very advanced manufacturing and assembly.

The studies ran between 1924 and 1932. Later, social scientist Fritz Roethlisberger and William Dickson, former head of personnel at Hawthorne, published a book called *Management and the Worker* based on all the research, which casts light back on Taylor's experiments.[18] This Hawthorne research and the conclusions drawn from it are widely known.

The first wave of Hawthorne experiments involved changing the physical environment – specifically changing the lighting for workers in an assembly area. With each lighting change, no matter how small, the researchers recorded an increase in productivity, *even* when the change involved making the lights dimmer again, including all the way back to their original setting.

The second wave of experiments involved a very small group of workers (five or six) who were sequestered in their own room away from the others to do their job of assembling relays. Over five years of experimentation, their working conditions were varied. Examples included the following:

- Giving them two 5-minute breaks (after a discussion with them about the best length of time) and then changing to two 10-minute breaks. Productivity increased, but when they received six 5-minute breaks, they disliked it, and output reduced.
- Providing food during breaks.
- Shortening the day by 30 minutes (output went up); shortening it further (output per hour went up, but overall output decreased); returning to the original day length (output peaked).

Various academics, notably Australian psychologist Elton Mayo, were drafted to advise the researchers, and it was Mayo who summarized the findings of the experiments. He argued that appreciating the workplace as a human system was important and that letting workers participate in decisions about their own work led to greater job satisfaction.

Workers are more productive, he implied, when they know they are being observed and that something is happening to them (the simplest form of what came to be called the *Hawthorne effect*). His conclusions from these small studies continue to have an impact on the way human relations management theory works today. Mayo's research was a turning point.

I tell this story again because although the results have regularly attracted scrutiny over the last 100 years, it was not until 2009 that the so-called Hawthorne effect was put under an appropriately strong microscope. We have economist Steven Levitt to thank for this. Professor Levitt of the University of Chicago is well known for cowriting the bestseller *Freako-nomics*. He is obsessively focused on using data to illuminate human behavior. In the case of the Hawthorne experiments, this proved important.

This is from the abstract of his paper, written with fellow Chicago economist John List, called "Was there really a Hawthorne effect at the Hawthorne plant?" They write, "The data from the first and most influential of these studies, the 'Illumination Experiment,' were never formally analyzed and were thought to have been destroyed. Our research has uncovered these data. Existing descriptions of supposedly remarkable data patterns prove to be entirely fictional."[19]

Entirely fictional. Levitt's analysis of the data is a comprehensive takedown (although it does allow for the possibility of a weak effect; that workers respond more to changes in manmade light than to fluctuations in natural light).

This is not the last time we will encounter research being used to draw enormous and influential conclusions despite the church-mouse poverty of the data it is based on.

It's practically impossible to imagine that Mayo and the Western Electric team had not diligently read Taylor's work. In fact, some of the research design features with the small group of women in his ball bearing inspection experiments are similar to those in the relay assembly experiments at Hawthorne (for example, the number of breaks taken each day, the duration of the breaks, allowing the workers to decide how many breaks to have).

Taylor gets no credit for this aspect of his work. It's easier just to categorize him as the theorist who cared only about efficiency and considered workers to be stupid and interchangeable. In fact, his data-rich approach to efficiency problems allowed not just for improvements in the use of shovels or reductions in the number of arm movements to lay a brick. Long before the Hawthorne effect, Taylor knew that the most important variable in efficiency equations was the human one.

I do not believe that Taylor was too concerned with making good jobs for the workers in his factories. But he was keen to eliminate bad jobs, where people earned less than they could because their productivity was low, worked inefficiently, performed identical tasks in randomly different ways, and did not achieve maximum prosperity for themselves or the firm. His assumptions were that everyone would want to be a "high-priced man" if they could be, and for those still with jobs at the conclusion of his assignments, greater prosperity would more than reward them for the harder work.

For him, each gang member was a unit of work experience, with both ability and desire to do more if it resulted in greater rewards. Taylor assumed each manager was there to design the job specification in detail and to measure the results, and would want, just as he had himself, to advance through the levels of management in the factory if given the chance.

What's Different About Knowledge Workers

To round out this historical context for the foundations of the professional management system, on which so many of our assumptions about work are still based today, I will briefly enlist the help of Peter Drucker.

There is a deep connection between Sloan, General Motors, and Drucker. Drucker had emigrated from his native Austria, first to England and then, in 1937, to the United States. His career as a business thinker took off in 1943, when Donaldson Brown, the man behind the administrative control system at GM, invited him in to conduct a kind of corporate health check of the company. Drucker attended every board meeting, interviewed employees, and analyzed production and decision-making processes.

The resulting book, *Concept of the Corporation*, popularized GM's multidivisional structure and led to articles, consulting engagements, and more books.[20] GM was apparently not thrilled with his output. Drucker suggested that the firm had to reexamine long-standing policies on customers, dealers, employees, and a lot more.

He wrote, "As to Sloan's decentralization of General Motors, it still stands—but it is becoming clear that it will have to be thought through again soon. Not only have the basic principles of his design been changed and revised so often that they have become fuzzy beyond recognition [...] and the individual makes of car from Chevrolet to Cadillac have also long ceased to represent major price classes the way Sloan originally designed them."

He went on, "Above all, Sloan designed a US company [...] but General Motors is clearly an international company today. It will survive and prosper only if it finds the right principles and the right organization for the multinational company."[21]

Fair enough. Sloan's original design was 20 years old by the time of Drucker's assignment: these days we do not expect our organizational models to last more than a few years; some are in a perpetual state of evolution. The book was a reputation maker for Drucker. Perhaps he felt some regrets at the reaction to his takedown of the mighty GM model. Sloan himself, Drucker later recalled, was so upset about the book that he "simply treated it as if it did not exist, never mentioning it and never allowing it to be mentioned in his presence."[22]

For Taylor and Sloan, their obsession as managers was efficiency – how to achieve it, how to maximize it, and how to turn it into prosperity. They did assume, because it was their norm, that every bricklayer, pig-iron carrier, industrial engineer, and buyer of car parts would want to improve their efficiency, to make more money, or to advance up the hierarchy in some way.

What Drucker understands, before anyone else, is that efficiency is the metric of the manual worker, but for this new creature in the world of business that he calls the *knowledge worker* (a term he coined in *The Effective Executive,* published in 1967),[23] effectiveness, not efficiency, is the better metric. Knowledge work cannot be defined by quantity of output nor by costs: it can be defined only by results.

Knowledge workers, particularly the executives Drucker was most interested in, are hard to manage and to measure. Most of the book is advice to executives on how to be as effective as possible. He has three simple and contemporary-sounding proposals:

- Make sure the executive job is well designed and is actually achievable (in other words, in an echo of Taylor, do not design jobs that only a superhuman could do).

- Make each executive job demanding in scale and scope.

- Start with what the individual can do, not with what the job requires.

Start, in other words, by designing *a good job*, based on individual strengths and motivations, and make personal strengths productive in service of firm objectives. It is no surprise that Drucker was already on to something that has taken another 50 years to become more mainstream.

In this mid-1960s book, Drucker critiqued the Western executive appraisal system for being too weakness-focused, and he contrasted the Japanese system of the time, which he considered 100% strengths based for the simple reason that in a system where you cannot be fired, why bother to focus on weaknesses?

Professional managers of the kind Alfred Sloan helped to define, still today, tend to be well-rounded, because the system rears them to be that way. The highest praise for an up-and-comer in a professional management organization is that they have "general manager potential." Their performance reviews spend as much time on their improvement needs as on their strengths. There are firms who operate differently, who focus more on the individual's distinctive capabilities and how to strengthen them even if other abilities remain undeveloped, but the old habits are hard to shake.

A quintessential example of professional management talent thinking is the Current Estimated Potential (CEP) system created at Royal Dutch/Shell Group more than 50 years ago and since adopted by other organizations.[24] Your CEP is defined as the current, realistic estimate of the highest job that an individual will be able to perform in their future career at Shell.

The system was designed on the one hand to help the firm identify future leaders and assess the state of the talent pool and, on the other hand, to deliver quality feedback to the individual about where they stand. With your first CEP rating delivered after three years, it was not a system designed for much of today's world, where the need for frequent reskilling to fill future jobs is common.

The talent norms of the professional management era were built on a foundation of predictable pathways through an organization, with bigger titles and higher rewards to those advancing up the hierarchy. If you were "general manager potential," you would be progressively moved further away from the frontline, in the broad direction of the executive ranks.

The norms and systems were designed to perpetuate the professional manager class. That was the promise of employment – to move you from "doer" to "manager of other doers," with spans and layers to support your elevation.

The New Norms

Times change. Eras come to an end, sometimes messily, as the old rules no longer seem to apply but the new playbook is not fully written. In this transition, the secular move from one business era to the next has been overlaid with a once-in-a-100-year global virus. For all its tragic consequences – the premature deaths, the family separations, the chronic sicknesses – businesses learned a lot under lockdown. Faced with sometimes total inability to operate "as normal," firms discovered sources of energy and creativity that kept things running right through the worst of times.

A communication line between leaders and the front lines, which had been structurally disconnected by professional management processes, was rapidly reestablished. I remember the Asia Pacific CEO of a global multinational explaining to me in late 2021 that his boss in the United States had simply started to pick up the phone to call the relevant person in China or Australia or Japan to get to the resolution of the day's new problem. We are making decisions in five or six hours that used to take five or six months, he said.

The need for a new solution to the problem of the "middle" in many firms was never clearer than during lockdown. The traditional professional management activity of Planning was suspended. For a period, plans did not matter, only actions. What made the actions possible during COVID-19 was the software of the organization – the human ability to communicate, collaborate, and solve problems – not the hardware, the org charts, and the formal levels of authority. In leadership meetings, as COVID-19 started to fade into the distance, the question was how to preserve the very best of lockdown behavior (smaller teams, faster ways of working, tighter connections between leaders and front lines) while still ensuring that all the right people were represented in the most critical decisions.

I have described the end of the trade-off between scale and intimacy in the way we think about customers. People management is the next battleground: it will not be immune from the same collapse. Scale and worker intimacy must now be delivered together.

While it is straightforward to project what type of leaders a firm will need based on competitive and strategic goals, it's hard to know what the individual will need if their motivations at work are unexplored and unexpressed. The assumption that everyone is always looking to move up, that all managers aspire to wider spans and more layers beneath them, is oversimplifying. The old model was to promote on capability without taking appetite for managerial responsibilities into account. Today, individual contributors are core to most organizations, and the choice to be one and to stay one is quite normal.

Just as we have long since understood the value of de-averaging our customers, so can we de-average workers in the hope of better understanding what is going to make them productive, satisfied, and retained. There are plenty of sophisticated chief human resource officers (CHROs) who understand this need well. It is no coincidence that the last decade – as we transition from one era to the next – has seen an explosion of creativity and innovation in talent management.

Supporting the innovations is a set of integrated software, platforms, and applications. There are – among others – tools for recruitment, onboarding, payroll, benefits administration, workforce planning, staffing, performance management, learning and development, organizational network analysis, employee engagement, and people analytics. Many solutions are now starting to include artificial intelligence.

These tools may come stand-alone or packaged in integrated human resource management systems (HRMSs) such as Peoplesoft (now owned by Oracle), Workday, and SAP SuccessFactors. These HRMSs have done a lot to automate many of the routine activities of HR teams in the name of efficiency. To do that, they make simplifying assumptions that allow a one-size-fits-all approach to many steps along the talent management value chain. These are professional management tools – Taylorist thinking updated for the working world that software ate.

What HRMSs also enable is people analytics, the *Moneyball* of organization management. At its best, people analytics can improve the reliability of predictions, for example, on workforce planning. At its worst, it may reduce people to nothing but data and ignore the richness of their motivations entirely.

An Explosion of Experiments

As we consider the innovations, we should start with the edge cases. Zappos, a direct-to-consumer shoe brand founded by the much-mourned Tony Hsieh, acquired by Amazon in 2009, adopted Holacracy, which emerged from the brain and persistence of Brian Robertson at Ternary Software in 2007 and bloomed into a rigorous system (with its own detailed "Constitution") that delegates decision authority, embeds self-management, and takes an axe to all hierarchy.[25]

Holacracy is organizational Marmite: you love it or you hate it. Zappos, with around 1,500 employees, is the still the largest firm we know that has embraced the system. Eighteen percent of its staff eventually took a voluntary redundancy offer rather than migrate to the new model almost 10 years ago. Still, that means more than 80% were at least fine with it.

We have seen similar programs before. Danish hearing-aid maker Oticon and its "Spaghetti Organization" of the 1990s – a novel way to think about project management – helped the small firm grow revenues for almost two decades and was intensively studied but later broke down with the increasing scale of the organization.[26]

Game designer and software distributor Valve makes a virtue of jettisoning all professional management conventions, including titles, hierarchies, job leveling, and reporting structures. Work on what you want to work on. The *New Employee Handbook* declares "We don't have any management, and nobody 'reports' to anybody else. We do have a founder/president, but even he isn't your manager." The desks at Valve have wheels. As the handbook says: "Think of those wheels as a symbolic reminder that you should always be considering where you could move yourself to be more valuable. But also think of those wheels as literal wheels, because that's what they are, and you'll be able to actually move your desk with them."[27]

Closer to the mainstream, firms like Netflix and Glassdoor replace "control" with "context," drastically reducing the employee rulebook, giving their salaried employees the freedom and responsibility to make more decisions for themselves, about how much vacation to take, for example, or what to put through on expenses.

Large incumbents like Accenture, Deloitte, and IBM replaced long-established performance management systems with new ones designed around nearer-term goals, more frequent feedback, and less focus on cross-calibration.

Many firms are looking to loosen the grip of functional silos using cross-functional teams, both temporary and persistent. Spotify invokes the medieval locker room to describe its working units: the squads, tribes, guilds, and chapters are a radical departure from traditional, functional organization designs, integrating multiple skills into a largely self-directing system where each squad decides what to build, how to build it, and how to make it interoperable with everything else in the app. You will not find a professional manager in their eight-person squads, the core organizational unit.[28]

Necessity is sometimes the mother of invention. At Bayer, the 160-year-old German maker of prescription drugs, agricultural products, and over-the-counter health remedies, a financial and operating performance crisis prompted the CEO to throw out the old norms and reimagine the firm's structure and ways of working.[29]

The plan laid out a reduction in management layers (from the current 12). Two billion euros of costs will be saved (much of it from head count reduction). Most striking, the main operating unit of the firm will become the self-managing team, somewhere between 5,000 to 6,000 of them, each with 15 to 20 team members. The teams will operate on a 90-day cycle, disbanding if their work is completed, reconfiguring or extending duration if deliverables are still outstanding. The changes are supposed to accelerate innovation and product development, speed up decision-making, and improve efficiency. The banner for the program is "Dynamic Shared Ownership," a term accompanied by a thesaurus of new titles and roles. At the time of writing, Bayer's 100,000 workers are only a handful of quarters into the change. This is the largest program of its kind currently under way. I, like many others, will be closely watching for progress reports on this particular new norms metamorphosis.

■　■　■

Some of the new norm changes I have described will turn out to be nothing more than fads, soon forgotten. Others have already become table stakes. So far, as so often, the gains have been uneven, with a few firms capturing major advantages from brilliant implementations of talent ideas that work for them; others following with their own experiments; and the rest still operating mainly with the old norms, wondering why it is so hard to find, keep, and grow the people they need.

Chapter 2

The Six Archetypes

Soon after World War II, the US Air Force began studying why American fighter pilots so often lost control of their planes. They suspected pilot error and poor training, but in time the real reason emerged. The cockpits had been designed using measurements of more than 4,000 pilots on 140 dimensions of size, including thumb length, crotch height, and distance from a pilot's eye to his ear, and then an average was calculated for each of these dimensions.

The snag was that this average-sized pilot didn't exist. Most men had one or more physical dimensions that differed significantly from the average. Their bodies fit awkwardly in the cockpit, making the plane difficult to control. The solution was to redesign cockpits with modifiable features, like adjustable seats.

We have a comparable problem in managing people at work. Fifty years ago, the average worker in a developed market was relatively easy to define. He was usually a man. He was usually the sole earner in the household. He probably traveled to his place of work every day. And he might reasonably expect to spend his entire career with one firm. This is not the average worker of today.

What Do You Want in a Job?

The de-averaging of workers begins with skills but cannot end there. Skills are fundamental – they are the building blocks for recruiting and talent development. But we knew, from just the first few dozen in-person interviews of our research, that we needed to layer in motivation to understand who people are at work.

After initial interviews and a review of historical approaches, we constructed a framework for motivations at work with these 10 dimensions:

- *Work centricity:* How much of my identity and sense of meaning comes from work?
- *Financial orientation:* How much does my level of income impact my happiness?
- *Future orientation:* Do I prioritize investing in a better future, or do I focus on living for today?
- *Status orientation:* How concerned am I about being perceived by others as successful?
- *Risk tolerance:* Am I willing to take risks to improve my life if I might end up worse off?
- *Variety:* Do I prefer change or predictability?
- *Autonomy:* How much do I value being in control of my own work?
- *Camaraderie:* Do I see work as primarily an individual or a team effort?
- *Mastery:* How much satisfaction do I find in the process of perfecting my craft?
- *Self-transcendence:* How important is it to me to make a positive difference in society?

Unlike some other approaches, which require forced-choice answers (you are either one thing or its opposite, with nothing in between), we shared a spectrum of possible responses with our workers. For example, on the dimension of work centricity, the people in our research see these two statements:

- My work is the main thing that defines who I am as a person.
- My work plays no part in defining who I am as a person.

They then select a response from a sliding scale. They might completely agree with the first bullet or completely agree with the second bullet, or they can pick from multiple points on the scale between the two.

We selected 19 countries, over three waves, in which to conduct the research. For the record, the countries were Canada, United States, Brazil, Finland, Norway, Denmark, Sweden, the United Kingdom, France, Germany, Italy, Saudi Arabia, United Arab Emirates, Nigeria, India, Japan, China, Indonesia, and Australia. Combined, they represent approximately 75% of global GDP. The group includes highly developed and wealthy countries, middle-income countries, and lower-income developing countries, from all parts of the world. In each, we surveyed a sample of approximately 2,000 individuals who represent the working population in all its diversity.

In five countries, we ran the quantitative survey twice, with approximately 2.5 years in between the samples, so that we could start to track changes and trends as the world of work moved past the COVID-19 pandemic. We also spent hundreds of hours on in-person interviews with workers of all types.

We found significant variation in job attribute rankings across countries, ages, and genders. Our first hypothesis, that – just as in cockpit design – constructing talent systems around the idea of an "average worker" is unlikely to meet the needs of any actual worker, was fully borne out.

The Six Worker Archetypes

From all the stories and data we collected, there emerged six distinct worker archetypes. Between them, they capture the motivations of all the workers in our research. The following sections describe the six, share comments from people talking about who they are at work, and illustrate the archetypes with descriptions of some well-known people whom I speculate each represent one of the archetypes. (We have not interviewed these people. I include them to help readers imagine the kind of person at work that each archetype represents.)

Givers

Givers find meaning in work that directly improves the lives of others. For them, work is about service. They are the archetype least motivated by money. They might gravitate toward caring professions such as medicine or teaching but can thrive in many lines of work where they directly interact with and help others. Their empathetic nature typically translates into a strong team spirit and deep personal relationships at work. Givers' more cautious nature means they tend to be forward planners, who may be hesitant to jump on new opportunities when they arise.

At their best, they are selfless, helping to build the trust every organization needs to function. At their worst, they may be impractical or naive.

> "I find deep joy in helping other people in all aspects of my life." – Analia, 45 years old, accounts payable manager, France

"There is a personal reward you get from helping other people, and it is faith driven for me." – Scott, 44 years old, consultant and soft skills trainer, United States

"I first started to work to support my husband and my family, but now I am doing it out of passion. It makes me really proud to support marginalized groups and help girls find their voice." – Eucharia, 48 years old, social worker for a nongovernmental organization (NGO), Nigeria

I've never met Oprah Winfrey, and chances are, I never will. Nonetheless, I would suggest that Oprah is a Giver. She is well known for her epically generous philanthropy, but it is her signature Oprah Angel Network that points to a Giver archetype. She created the network in 1998 and wound it up in 2010 when her TV show finished. It was in all respects a charity focused on donating money, often to organizations supporting underserved women and children around the world. It is an unambiguous example of her desire to help others thrive (most of the money came from her). But its origin story reveals a motivation that was just as much about role-modeling Giver behavior. In 1994 a nine-year-old girl wrote to Oprah about her efforts to collect small change in a bucket, which resulted in her raising $1,000. Oprah's reaction was, if a nine-year-old girl can do that, what could America's most famous talk show host do? She used her platform to inspire the general public (and later, many celebrities) to use their expertise, their talent, and their time to help others thrive – for example, building schools around the world and sending students to college who otherwise would not have been able to attend.

Operators

Operators find meaning and self-worth primarily outside of their jobs. They see work as a means to an end. They're not particularly motivated by status or autonomy and generally don't seek to stand out in their workplace. They prefer stability and predictability. Operators typically do not demand a sense of purpose from their company, often viewing their jobs in more transactional terms. At the same time, Operators are one of the most team-oriented archetypes and often see many of their colleagues as friends.

At their best, they are team players that form the dependable backbone of the organization. At their worst, they may be disengaged and lack proactivity.

> "I do enjoy being good at my job, but I don't necessarily get self-pride from it." – Caden, 18 years old, welder/fitter, United States
>
> "Before anything, I am a Mum. I work in my current job to be able to feed my family, but I would like to set up my own shop." – Mary, 29 years old, cleaner and shop assistant, Nigeria
>
> "I like where I work. But I try to keep it separate from my personal life—my family takes precedence over anything else." – Gaurav, 38 years old, regional sales manager at a ceramic tile company, India
>
> "My ranking is family, friends, work—work is just to live." – Juan, 23 years old, class teacher at Early Education Centre, China

It's harder to find real-life examples of Operators who are also in the public eye. By definition, they prefer to keep a low profile and frequently look at work as something important but not the definition of who they are; it's a place to make great friends but not a place to look for answers to the big questions of life. I recognize that he has had a long life and his archetype may well have evolved over time, but Warren Buffet, CEO of investment firm Berkshire Hathaway, presents with the core Operator characteristics.

Buffett leads a famously modest life. He lives in the same house in Omaha, Nebraska, that he purchased in 1958 for $31,500. He drives a 2014 Cadillac XTS, enjoys simple meals like hamburgers and Coca-Cola, and avoids ostentatious displays of wealth.

He is also famously conservative in his investment philosophy, favoring long-term investments in companies with predictable earnings: this is risk minimizing and puts high value on predictability. He is evidently passionate about investing but seems to view it primarily as a vehicle to achieve broader goals, such as philanthropy and financial stability for his shareholders.

His daily routine is simple and consistent. He spends a large part of his day reading and analyzing potential investments, as he has for decades. This is textbook Operator behavior. He prizes long-term relationships at work and often speaks highly of his partnerships, especially his 60-year collaboration with Charlie Munger. For all his success, he presents as humbly pragmatic, focused on value creation and sound investment principles, rather than seeking personal fulfillment or a grand sense of purpose from his role as CEO.

Artisans

Artisans seek out work that fascinates and inspires them. They are motivated by the pursuit of mastery and are always on the lookout to perfect their skills – for them, learning is lifelong.

They enjoy being valued for their expertise, although they are less concerned with status in the broader sense. Artisans typically desire a high degree of autonomy to practice their craft, and of all the archetypes, they place the least importance on camaraderie at work.

At their best, they can solve even the most complex of challenges. At their worst, they may seem aloof and lose sight of bigger objectives.

> "I love learning new abilities; I am always tuned on the new technology in my sector and try to use it to prospect and impress my clients; my employees call me 'High Tech Wagner.'" – Wagner, 60 years old, owner of a construction company, Brazil
>
> "Learning new things, and constantly reviewing and reflecting on myself, is my attitude toward work." – Jun, 36 years old, sales manager for consumer packaged goods, China
>
> "What matters the most to me in a job is excellence." – Kate, 45 years old, accountant for a government department, Nigeria

Jiro Ono is 98 years old and possibly both the best and the best-known sushi chef in the world. He moved to Tokyo to apprentice as a very young boy, became a certified sushi chef in 1951, and opened his 10-seat restaurant, Sukiyabashi Jiro, in 1965, below ground in the Ginza Tokyo Metro station. It is only very recently that poor health has forced him to step away from the counter. His son Yoshikazu now runs the restaurant. We know a lot about Jiro from an unusual 2011 documentary film, *Jiro Dreams of Sushi*. It is a homage to an

Artisan. The Japanese word *shokunin* carries with it both the sense of aspiring to mastery but also an utter dedication to producing the highest quality work. As Jiro explains in the film, he does the same thing every day over and over again and always wants to improve. He has a continuous yearning to achieve more, will never achieve perfection, but derives total satisfaction from its pursuit.

Explorers

Explorers value freedom and experiences. They tend to live in the present and seek out careers that provide a high degree of variety and excitement. Explorers place a higher than average importance on autonomy. They are also more willing than others to trade security for flexibility. They don't rely on their job for a sense of identity, often exploring multiple occupations during their lifetime. Explorers tend to adopt a pragmatic approach to professional development, obtaining only the level of expertise they think they need.

At their best, they will enthusiastically throw themselves at whatever task is required of them. At their worst, they may be directionless and lack conviction.

> "I love my job, and I love the fact that things change all the time." – Beatrice, 50 years old, runs a textile manufacturing company, France
>
> "I changed my job from a hotel manager to courier customer service manager because I think there is more training and growth, and I attach great importance to {…} the space for learning." – Shuang, 30 years old, customer service manager at a courier, China

"I don't want to leave my job, but I want to study to open new doors; I have already studied law, and I want to take other courses: IT, informatics, theology." – Cristiane, 44 years old, coordinator for a Legal Association, Brazil

Arianna Huffington, the Greek American author of 15 books, syndicated columnist, sleep expert, wellness advocate, and media entrepreneur, has built a career through multiple industries. Her journey is testament to the intellectual curiosity, adaptability, and embrace of variety that epitomizes the Explorer.

Born in Greece, Huffington immigrated to England as a teenager and studied economics at Cambridge University where she was the first foreign-born president of the Cambridge Union debating society. She had some early TV experience, co-hosting the BBC talk and entertainment show *Saturday Night at the Mill*. Moving to New York in 1980 launched her political career. She worked as a writer and commentator, advocating for small government and limited welfare programs. This culminated in an unsuccessful run for California governor in the 2003 recall election.

Huffington became interested in entrepreneurial ventures. In 2005, she cofounded *The Huffington Post* (now HuffPost), one of the early online news aggregators and blogging platforms. She was also its editor-in-chief.

In 2016, she left HuffPost in another transformative career pivot to launch Thrive Global, a health and wellness company. Huffington channeled her own experience with exhaustion (she famously collapsed from overwork in 2007) into Thrive Global's mission to promote mindfulness, good sleep habits, and a balanced approach to work-life integration.

Strivers

Strivers have a strong desire to make something of themselves. They are motivated by professional success and value status and compensation. They are forward planners who can be relatively risk averse, opting for well-trodden paths to success. Strivers are willing to tolerate less variety so long as it is in service of their longer-term goals. They tend to define success in relative terms and thus can be more competitive and transactional in their relationships than most other archetypes.

At their best, they are disciplined and transparent. At their worst, their competitiveness may degrade trust and camaraderie at work.

> "I consider myself as quite ambitious. I enjoy rubbing elbows with other people working for the district, I like having good things said about my name, and I want to move into higher up positions." – Sofia, 30 years old, school secretary to a high school vice principal, United States
>
> "What matters to me is to have a prominent role in my team, be very professional, and demonstrate my ability to do my job really well." – Alton, 23 years old, corporate banking analyst, United States
>
> "I aspire to do well and better than most of my peers, as there is a lot of competition now if you want to climb up the corporate ladder. I try and learn new things to stay ahead of the pack." – Amit, 43 years old, chief sales officer at multinational tech services firm, India
>
> "If I see that my peers are more successful than me, I will use this to motivate myself and work very hard to close the gap." – Caifa, 47 years old, tech company CEO, China

There is one version of the Striver that spends most of their career with one firm and rises to more and more senior positions with time and increasing capability. Tricia Griffith, president and CEO of the Progressive Corporation, joined the firm as a claims representative in 1988. Doug McMillon, president and CEO of Walmart, had his first role at the firm in 1984 when he was a teenage summer intern, unloading trucks at a distribution center. Mary Barra, chair and CEO of General Motors, was first employed there in 1980 as a co-op student, when her role was checking fenders and hoods. David Taylor, former CEO and former executive chair of Proctor & Gamble, spent 40 years at the firm. Ursula Burns, former CEO and former chair of Xerox, started at Xerox as a summer intern and stayed for 37 years. Makiko Ono, CEO of Suntory Beverage & Food, has spent her entire 40-year career there.

This list is not to suggest that only "lifers" have a strong chance of being Strivers and of making it to the highest levels in a firm. Strivers switch firms just like other archetypes. For those who do stay put, it is because their firm continues to offer them the right combination of challenge, recognition, risk, and reward, and because they value the two-way benefits of loyalty.

Pioneers

Pioneers are on a mission to change the world. They form strong views on the way things should be and seek out the control necessary to achieve that vision. They are the most risk-tolerant and future-oriented of all the archetypes. Pioneers identify profoundly with their work. Their vision matters more than anything, and they are willing to make great personal sacrifices in its pursuit. Their work relationships tend to be more transactional in nature. Their vision is often at least partly altruistic, but it is distinctly their own.

At their best, they mobilize their infectious energy to bring about change. At their worst, they may be uncompromising and imperious.

> "I have been a rebel since my childhood. I love having autonomy on the decisions that I take and that drive my career choices." – Ami, 32 years old, founder of a training solutions company, India
>
> "I am a person who is willing to take risks and bear the consequences." – Yanlan, 32 years old, salesperson for a home decoration company, China
>
> "I am very comfortable taking risks. I chose to have a kid by myself, and I have gone for jobs that felt like a big stretch." – Tammy, 49 years old, innovation manager at a medical devices company, United States
>
> "My plan is to manufacture my own products with my own name. It will go viral and will be very popular. That's my main goal." – Ifechukwu, 22 years old, electrician, Nigeria

Yvon Chouinard, born in 1938, is a climber, surfer, falconer, and environmentalist who, through his company Patagonia, has redefined what a successful, high-impact business can be.

Chouinard's love for the outdoors began early. Growing up in Maine, he was drawn to the challenge and beauty of climbing. He developed a reputation for fearless ascents. Frustrated by the quality of climbing equipment available, he became a blacksmith so he could forge his own pitons, the metal spikes that were traditionally used to anchor climbers and protect them from a fall. This desire for better gear sparked his entrepreneurial ambition.

Chouinard started selling his climbing equipment in stores, eventually shifting to mail-order sales. His focus on high-quality, innovative gear was popular with climbers. He was already an advocate for clean climbing practices and became concerned about the environmental impact of pitons left behind on rock faces. This led him to develop less destructive climbing techniques and introduce reusable gear options.

In the 1970s, he expanded into outdoor apparel, and Patagonia was born. The company's mission – to build the best product, cause no unnecessary harm, and use business to inspire and implement solutions to the environmental crisis – reflected Chouinard's values from the outset.

Patagonia's commitment to environmentalism goes beyond product design. The company donates a significant portion of its profits to environmental causes, supports grassroots activism, and advocates for sustainable business practices. Chouinard has personally been a critic of environmental degradation and a champion for responsible resource management.

He built a successful business not just by selling products but by aligning his company with a greater ambition: to protect the natural world. Through innovation, activism, and a commitment to ethical practices, Patagonia has become a model for businesses that strive to be both profitable and environmentally responsible. In 2022, Chouinard took the revolutionary step of transferring ownership of Patagonia to a trust dedicated to fighting climate change: the firm's environmental mission will continue for generations to come.[1]

Archetypes Around the World

No archetype is better or worse than any other. While a firm made up only of Operators might lack dynamism, one packed only with Strivers and Pioneers might collapse under the weight of conflicting egos. Each brings a unique contribution.

It's also important to recognize that while some workers present clearly as a singular archetype, the line can be blurrier for others. Their distinctive set of attitudes may position them somewhere between two – or potentially even more – of the profiles. As you will see later, archetypes may also change over the course of a lifetime, as events and environments continue to shape workers throughout their careers.

At the intersection of archetypes and countries, we find a remarkably consistent mix across the world. In every country, Operators and Strivers are the two largest archetypes – combined, they consistently represent 40–50% of the working population.

As you can see in Figure 2.1:

- Operators are on average 24% of the working population (lowest in Nigeria at 17%, highest in the United Kingdom and China at 28%).

- Strivers are on average 21% (lowest in Indonesia at 16%, highest in Japan at 29%).

- The next largest archetype is Givers, on average 17% (lowest in Finland at 8%, highest in Saudi Arabia at 24%).

	Global	Lowest mix		Highest mix	
Archetype	% of workforce	Country	% of workforce	Country	% of workforce
Operator	24%	Nigeria	17%	UK, China	28%
Striver	21%	Indonesia	16%	Japan	29%
Artisan	17%	Nigeria	9%	Finland	28%
Giver	17%	Finland	8%	Saudi Arabia	24%
Explorer	11%	Japan, Italy, Australia	9%	Finland	15%
Pioneer	10%	Sweden, France	7%	Nigeria	23%

Figure 2.1 The intersection of archetypes and countries.

The Six Archetypes

- Then come Artisans, on average also 17% (lowest in Nigeria at 9%, highest in Finland at 28%).

- Then come Explorers, on average 11% (lowest in Japan, Italy, and Australia at 9%, highest in Finland at 15%).

- Finally, Pioneers make up on average 10% (lowest in France and Sweden at 7%, highest in Nigeria at 23%).

Just as there is a rich diversity of archetypes across countries, there is also variety across job types. We are able to classify our workers into broad categories of employment (Manual, Service, Administration, Care, and Knowledge), and we observed that all archetypes are present in all types of employment.

There are some high-level trends as well:

- Manual workers, for example in manufacturing, construction, maintenance, and logistics, are more likely to be Operators and Artisans.

- Administrative workers, for example in clerical and secretarial jobs, are more likely to be Operators and less likely to be Pioneers.

- Care workers, for example in healthcare and education, are more likely to be Givers.

- Explorers may gravitate toward occupations in Service, such as hospitality, sales, and personal services.

- Strivers and Pioneers may be drawn to Knowledge roles, management roles, professional services, and technical occupations.

We also know that life stage and education have material impacts on archetype. We designed our research to understand how archetypes might change with age. And we see that for some people, they do. Some people are who they are at work, over their entire career. But a typical progression with aging is for Pioneers and Strivers when young to become Givers and Artisans when older. You'll read about this in more detail in Chapter 6.

The more education a worker completes, the more likely they are to score higher on autonomy, future orientation, status orientation, and self-transcendence. This translates into a higher share of Pioneers and Strivers and a lower share of Operators.

Take the United States as an example: among workers with a bachelor's degree or higher, 11% are Pioneers and 24% Strivers. For those with a high school qualification or less, it's 7% and 16%, respectively – a 50% + difference for both.

The Most Important Job Attributes

Let's return to the questions the chapter opened with: Why do you go to work? Who are you when you get there? We can see the shape of each archetype emerge in their rankings of job attributes.

You might expect that cultures, climates, demographics, wealth levels, and prevailing economic conditions would make a difference to the ways people feel about work. It turns out, the variation between countries is far less than the variation within them.

Globally, the most important attributes workers look for in a job are as follows, in order:

1. Good compensation
2. Flexibility/good hours
3. Interesting work

4. Good relationship with coworkers

5. Job security

6. Learning and growth

7. Job that's helpful to society

8. Autonomy

9. Company that inspires me

10. Prestige

Good compensation is ranked first in 15 of the 19 countries. The exceptions are France, Denmark, Norway, and Finland. There, the most important attribute is *interesting work*, with *good compensation* second in the ranking. It's not hard to imagine why, in these four wealthy countries, which offer high incomes, well-developed state-sponsored social programs, and safety nets, that good compensation could be of lesser importance.

Contrast this with Japan, where good compensation is ranked higher than in any other country in our research. Thirty years of wage stagnation, a relatively unstable employment market (with 40% of Japanese workers in nonregular employment), and a very low national investment in people development (one twentieth of what the United States spends per person) – again, it is not hard to understand the extreme importance of compensation.

In countries with younger populations, enjoying the economic tailwind of a demographic dividend, we are not surprised to see *learning and growth* much more highly valued than on average. This group includes middle-income countries like India (median age 28 years), Indonesia (29), Nigeria (17), and Brazil (32), as well as also rich countries like Saudi Arabia (29) and the United Arab Emirates (33). In each of these, *learning and growth* is the second most important job attribute.

By contrast, in the United Kingdom (median age 40 years), Australia (38), Japan (48), Germany (45), and France (42), *learning and growth* is much less important.

Putting it simply, *learning and growth* is a top job attribute in all of the developing markets but in none of the developed markets. In a working world that will see greater and greater emphasis on re-skilling and up-skilling over the course of a career, a workforce that prizes their own development will be an asset.

Chapter 6 explores the implications of having more older people in the workforce. For now, note the connection between a younger workforce, high scores on learning and growth, a high mix of the more risk-tolerant Explorers and Pioneers, and a lower mix of Operators.

Likewise on *flexibility*, the number-two job attribute in the global ranking. In wealthier, developed countries like Denmark, the United Kingdom, Australia, and the United States, flexibility is materially more important than on average. Whereas in low-income India, for example, it's much less important, while *job security* is much more important than elsewhere.

Some countries are too geographically diverse to be looked at as a single whole, and we have tried to take that into account. For example, in China, workers in Tier 1 cities score much higher on risk tolerance than the population as a whole, which shows up as a higher share of Pioneers. In France, financial orientation is higher in Paris than the rest of the country, increasing the share of Strivers in the capital.

One last observation about countries: the importance of *autonomy* at work varies widely around the world, from much higher than the global average in Japan, Sweden, Finland, Italy, and France to much lower than the global average in Nigeria, Indonesia, and India. As you will see, part of this difference is explained by the mix of older workers in the population: they highly value autonomy.

Which Job Attributes Does Each Archetype Value Most?

The research allows us to study the importance of job attributes along multiple dimensions.

One of the most important dimensions was to consider the job attribute rankings of the six archetypes. What first jumps out is that *all* archetypes rate *good compensation* as their number-one most important attribute.

For Strivers, it's overwhelmingly the most important:

> "I need to work 14 hours a day to be happy. I enjoy the pressure and having many responsibilities. Money is important but as important is getting recognition from my boss and having a strong impact." – Christophe, 60 years old, head of human resources (HR) and operations for a media company, France, Striver
>
> "It is very important that you have a plan and control over your own future. I feel that I am not qualified to take risks. Promotion and salary increase can motivate me most." – Jie, 24 years old, data analyst at high-speed rail company, China, Striver

For Operators and Givers, a strong desire for camaraderie translates into a high ranking for good relationships with coworkers:

> "When I look for a new job, I focus first on what matters to me. What I do for work, it feels like I do it for volunteering and I happen to get paid. […] A job is your family." – Holly, 61 years old, executive

administrative coordinator for a legal services consortium, United States, Operator

"I get high satisfaction in helping and counseling people and helping them in fighting adversities." – Rekhaa, 59 years old, principal at a private school, India, Giver

For Artisans, by contrast, work relationships are far less important. What Artisans value higher than others is doing work they find interesting:

"I could be doing something else that paid more, but this is what I love to do. I want to keep broadening my knowledge about nails and manicures to offer more services to my clients." – Samanta, 42 years old, manicurist, Brazil, Artisan

"I chose this field because I have always been passionate about research and agriculture to help people be self-sufficient and improve their resources. I am very passionate about what I do, and I feel I have become an expert in my field . . . I want to work for another 20 years!" – Alphonsus, 58 years old, university researcher on agriculture, Nigeria, Artisan

For Pioneers, flexibility is much less important than for the average worker. Remember, they are planning to change the world:

"I had to make large investments to open my own business; I took a risk, and it worked out well for me. If it hadn't been successful, I would have to take another risk." – Danilda, 43 years old, events decorator, Brazil, Pioneer

Likewise, for Explorers, job security is less important than for others. They know they may be moving on to something new before long:

> "I've had five different jobs in the past 10 years. If I'm not happy with my day-to-day job, then I will do something about it." – Christopher, 33 years old, senior manager of consumer insights for multinational food services company, France, Explorer

This leads to an important distinction between job attributes and job satisfaction.

We know which attributes are most important when people think about a job. We know how well they believe their current job is delivering against the attributes. They also tell us how satisfied or dissatisfied they are with the current job and how likely or unlikely they are to want to stay in it.

We can use simple statistical tools to understand which of the 10 attributes are most associated with an individual's satisfaction at work and their intention to stay in a job. I say "associated with" because we cannot be sure that one thing precisely causes the other, only that they are associated in a statistically significant way.

When we run the analyses, we see that when it comes to job satisfaction, good compensation and flexibility drop outside the top three factors, less important than interesting work, an inspirational company, and good relationships with colleagues. Pay and benefits are critical but on their own do not create a satisfied worker.

When we then look at these same results for each archetype, good compensation is highly correlated with job satisfaction for three of our six. By now, you can probably guess which three.

If you guessed Strivers, Pioneers, and Operators, you are absolutely right.

Strivers value compensation and the recognition that comes with promotions and milestone achievements (which are themselves associated with higher compensation). Pioneers value compensation as a way to stay sufficiently independent so that they can keep pursuing their dreams to change the world. Operators value compensation as the way to ensure they can fund the thing they care most about (their life outside work).

By contrast, compensation is not a top three factor when it comes to satisfaction for Givers, Artisans, or Explorers. For these archetypes, interesting work, an inspiring company, and good relationships with colleagues are much more predictive.

When we came to repeat the research, in early 2024, we found little change in archetype mix. The job attributes ranking in 2024 looks much as it did in earlier waves.

This lack of change is striking: in the first waves we asked whether the COVID-19 pandemic was causing people to rethink their work-life balance, and around 60% said it was. The proportion was even higher in Nigeria, Indonesia, Brazil, India, and China.

Perhaps COVID-19 changed a lot about *how* we work (for some, if not for all) but changed much less about *why* we work. Perhaps the sugar-rush of quiet quitting, and actual quitting, was enabled mainly by government subsidies during the worst of the pandemic, and that once those went away, people wanted and needed to get back to work.

Are Archetypes Valuable at Work?

Do we need archetypes? There are those who object to any type of system that labels humans, arguing that it constrains more than it explains and that it ends up limiting people's perception of each other to their type rather than for the capabilities and true potential they possess.

One of the most widely used typing systems is the Myers-Briggs Type Indicator (MBTI). *What's Your Type?* by Professor Merve Emre, published in 2019, delves into the history and impact of MBTI. Emre explores the origins of the test, its creators, and its influence on aspects of society, including the workplace, relationships, and self-identity.[2]

The book begins by introducing Katherine Briggs and her daughter Isabel Myers, the two women behind the development of MBTI. Emre reveals their motivations, their influences, and the cultural context in which they created the test 80 years ago, drawing attention to their interest in the work of Carl Jung and their desire to categorize and understand people's personalities using Jung's psychological types.

Emre argues that despite its widespread use and popularity, the MBTI test lacks scientific validity and reliability. It relies on subjective interpretations and a binary categorization system that oversimplifies the complexity of human personalities.

MBTI makes three claims about its test: it will reveal your true type, your type will cause differences in your behavior, and your type will never change. You are what the test says you are, and for life, because your type is inborn. In the view of Emre and other commentators, this fails to capture the dynamic nature of human behavior and the context-dependent nature of personality traits.

Emre explores MBTI's integration into institutions, including corporations and educational settings, and argues that it has been marketed as a tool for self-improvement and personal development, but its limitations and oversights have been overlooked.

The binary nature of MBTI, with its emphasis on opposites such as introversion/extroversion and thinking/feeling, has led to the perpetuation of gender norms and expectations, Emre says, and this can stifle an individual's understanding and expression of their true self.

Throughout her book, she also questions the ethical implications of MBTI's use in employment and hiring. She criticizes the widespread reliance on the test for personnel decisions, arguing that it can lead to discrimination and bias. The rigid categorization enforced by your MBTI may result in individuals being overlooked or pigeonholed based on their type, rather than their actual qualifications and capabilities.

There is broad agreement with these concerns. Academics Randy Stein and Alexander B. Swan describe the problem this way: "The central premises of the MBTI theory include that people belong to a 'true' personality 'type', that 'type' causes differences in observed behavior, and that 'type' is determined at birth.[3] For the MBTI theory to be correct, each of these three claims needs to be supported."[4] They go on to explain that none of those three claims is well supported.

Just as important, as we began to see the six archetypes emerge from the data, was another topic Stein and Swan raise ". . . given the rather complex nature of the MBTI theory (the very detailed descriptions of the four dichotomies, and the layers of dominant, secondary, and auxiliary functions), it is difficult to see how end users . . . would be able to generate accurate on-the-spot self-typing of their 'unconscious' self."[5]

We have made it a priority to keep our archetypes simple and few, yet comprehensive.

Many organizations use some version of an MBTI test to assess candidates applying for jobs. The thought is that by estimating which traits are likely to be most important in a specific role, the hiring team can make better decisions about candidates when they know their personality profile. There is, however, plenty of countervailing evidence. Where MBTI asserts the fixed nature of an individual's type, there is newer research suggesting traits can vary significantly in the same person depending on time of day, for example, or the physical environment or whether they are currently employed or unemployed.

Our overall approach to archetypes – both what they are and how they can be used – is different.

We are completely focused on people at work. No doubt, there are ties between work life and nonwork life, but it is not our remit to try to explain humans in their entirety.

We are quite certain that archetypes are not fixed at birth. They can evolve with time and with changes in job situations.

We do not believe the archetype is a *test*. It's an assistant, a shorthand guide to help you understand who you are at work and what makes you thrive when you get there. The value is for you to gain deeper insight into why you feel fulfilled, recognized, and rewarded at work, or why you don't, and to provide a language to discuss your motivations with colleagues and bosses.

There is also value for the firm, as there has to be. Firms of scale include many archetypes in their workforce. Most will have all six. The new insights on motivations allow leaders to redesign the way they help workers achieve their potential, while staying focused on business objectives.

Archetype thinking proves its value if it helps in the design of good jobs. Most jobs have elements that are highly inflexible: in the language of Taylor and Drucker, the output or the expected results are fixed. There are flexible elements too. For knowledge workers these might include where the work is done or who to collaborate with. For blue-collar workers, so critical in many industries around the world, many firms, at least in developed markets, are moving past traditional models of strict hours and fixed schedules, with flexible shift-rostering and shorter work weeks, or perhaps with the deployment of connected worker software platforms that provide real-time collaboration between frontline teams, even ones in different locations.

While fixed job elements may not be altered, the flexible elements can be adjusted to line up with individual motivations. We would not expect an Artisan to flourish in a role where success demands round-the-clock team interaction; some protected time for individual work will be important. We would not expect an Explorer to thrive in a role with highly repetitive tasks and limited interaction with other team members, nor an Operator to flourish in an unstructured role with vague deliverables and unpredictable working hours, nor a Giver to be satisfied with an appraisal system that offers no recognition of culture-building and team experience.

These insights are individual and also team-level. If we want teams composed of a mix of archetypes to be high-performing, we need self-awareness and other awareness from all team members, especially the leaders.

We have come to believe that there is no perfect mix of archetypes for a firm or function. The tool should not be used to try to compare your mix to a theoretically better one. There are simply too many variables: country, age, size, industry sector, competitive position – to name just a few.

Other type indicator systems have a different perspective on the mix topic. You will find yards of discussion threads on Quora and Reddit and WeChat on questions like "What is the perfect MBTI mix for my [innovation, or marketing, or start up, etc.] project?" This approach makes two assumptions: that people can understand the interactions between each of the 16 MBTI types and all the others, and that there is one magical combination just right for a particular activity.

The six worker archetypes are not built that way. They are a reliable, data-driven shorthand for people to understand themselves and their colleagues at work without the false precision that comes with forced-choice questions (you are either *this* or *that*, but not a bit of both, or either depending on the situation) and without overcomplexity. Archetypes will help teams function more effectively, but they are not an input for team member selection.

Most firms are continuously refining their workforce through re-skilling, external hiring, and internal development. As far as archetypes go, you have what you have. It's a function of your history, what you say about your firm in recruiting, and how you manage your workers once they join.

We think people want to understand themselves at work and that it's natural and positive to want a language to anchor work attitudes. Firms must be careful in implementation – the cartoons of the archetypes could easily be negative: Strivers are sharp-elbowed corporate animals, Explorers are fickle and can't keep a job, Artisans are bad team players, and so on. But after hundreds of conversations with people leaders and hearing from tens of thousands of workers, we are convinced the benefits of understanding our individual motivations outweigh any concerns.

Work encompasses such a wide range of human activity. Assuming the forecasts are right, we are opening another chapter in the human/work relationship, with the rapid growth of artificial intelligence applications. At the same time, the concept of the individual with a unique identity, although relatively new, is more and more central. It's a post-Enlightenment assertion that we are each different and entitled to the right to be unique, to pursue the things that uniquely motivate us.

Archetypes turn a traditionally one-way dialog about career planning ("This is what we see ahead for you" and "these are the skills you need to develop next") into a two-way discussion that both firm and individual own, where skills are still central, but mindset and motivations are understood and included too.

Using Your Archetype

It is our belief that, with workers trained and aware of their own and the other five archetypes, everyone at work can find a way to collaborate effectively with their colleagues.

That said, there are all kinds of possible conflicts to navigate. There can be interpersonal conflicts related to work styles, for example. There can be role conflicts, where ambiguities in role definitions or overloaded employees conflict over expectations and deliverables. There can be values conflicts, disagreements over what is right and wrong at work, some of which might originate in cultural differences. And there can be power conflicts, where differences in status lead to feelings of disrespect or of authority undermined.

Archetype knowledge is a powerful defense against each of these, and it's a useful tool if conflict does break out.

First, here's a quick recap of the six archetypes:

- *Givers:* Driven by helping others; thrive in collaborative environments
- *Operators:* Value stability and teamwork; prefer clear instructions and minimal risks

- *Explorers:* Seek variety, creativity, and new experiences; prefer flexibility and innovation

- *Artisans:* Motivated by mastery and pride in their work; prefer autonomy and focus on quality

- *Strivers:* Ambitious and career-oriented; motivated by recognition and advancement

- *Pioneers:* Visionary and entrepreneurial; driven by creating and sometimes leading new ventures

The 10 Most Common Conflicts

In what follows, I describe 10 archetype conflicts. This may not be the full list. These are simply the ones that I have observed most often.

Operators Versus Explorers or Pioneers

Shows up as: routines versus innovation. Operators might find the constant changes proposed by Explorers and Pioneers to be exhausting and disruptive, while they might see Operators as resistant to necessary innovation.

Steps to mitigate: Explorers/Pioneers, increase your communication frequency about upcoming changes. Avoid the "big-bang" change announcement. Design incremental changes on the journey if possible. Operators, you need to ask more questions, listen carefully, see if the changes can be incorporated into existing routines.

Givers Versus Strivers

Shows up as: Collaboration versus competition. Givers might see Strivers as competitive and self-absorbed, whereas Strivers might see Givers as lacking ambition.

Steps to mitigate: Givers, your role (and satisfaction) is helping others thrive. That includes Strivers. Find ways to align Strivers' personal goals with team objectives. Channel their competitive energy toward collective success. Strivers, give more credit to the Givers who have helped you achieve your milestones.

Explorers Versus Artisans

Shows up as: Flexibility versus quality. The Explorer's desire for variety and pursuit of novelty can clash with the Artisan's focus on meticulous, high-quality work. Artisans can see Explorers as unfocused, even disruptive.

Steps to mitigate: Explorers, you have to make the case to the team with concrete examples of how flexibility and new approaches can benefit everyone. Collaborate on pilots or micro-implementations that show how innovation will not compromise quality standards. Artisans, force yourself to stay open to new approaches, and help Explorers on implementation work, ensuring innovative ideas are executed with precision and quality.

Pioneers Versus Givers

Shows up as: Leading change versus helping others. The Pioneer's drive for an entrepreneurial approach can clash with the Giver's need for support and collaboration. Pioneers feel restrained by the Giver's practical demands.

Steps to mitigate: Pioneers, involve Givers early. Give them time to develop ways to incorporate new ideas, or new business models, into their plans for an integrated team success. Givers can be highly effective communication bridges between Pioneers and other team members, helping everyone to see the potential value of a new direction.

Strivers Versus Pioneers

Shows up as: Personal progress versus vision. The ambitions and focus on advancement of the Striver can conflict with the Pioneer's "big vision," which has uncertainties in it. Strivers can see Pioneers as impractical, while Pioneers see Strivers as too individualistic.

Steps to mitigate: Pioneers can be good mentors for Strivers, helping them to see the opportunities that the "big vision" creates for goal-driven Strivers. They are both driven by achievement. Once Strivers understand and align with the vision, they can set personal goals that line up their individual success with the organization's. And as in their tensions with Givers, Strivers would do well to recognize the contributions of the Pioneers as they celebrate.

Artisans Versus Pioneers

Shows up as: Mastery and quality versus change. As in the Artisan conflict with Explorers, so with Pioneers. Artisans see the Pioneer's drive for new methods and new ideas to be at odds with their drive for the highest quality work. They can see Pioneers as shallow. Pioneers see Artisans prioritizing perfection over progress.

Steps to mitigate: Artisans, stick up for your emphasis on quality and mastery of the craft. But also make it part of your mastery journey to incorporate new approaches and work techniques, not only to cling tight to the old ways. Pioneers, remember that even new ideas need the high-quality execution that Artisans thrive on.

Operators Versus Strivers

Shows up as: Stability versus ambition. While both archetypes are not risk-seekers at work, the Striver's ambition will create deadline and deliverable pressures on the Operator, who much prefers a stable routine. Operators can look at Strivers as complacent.

Steps to mitigate: Operators, you need to help Strivers see their paths for advancement using the existing structure and ways of working. Make it easy for Strivers to lead within the already defined boundaries around the work. Strivers, respect the process, and ask Operators for advice on problem-solving which uses their systems and processes knowledge.

Explorers Versus Strivers

Shows up as: Creativity versus achievement. Strivers seem too conventional to Explorers, which they associate with a stifling of innovation. Strivers look at Explorers as impractical and insufficiently committed to delivering results now.

Steps to mitigate: Explorers, you have to make the case that innovative projects can have clear goals and measurable results. Strivers, if you think it through, you have much to learn from Explorers in the way their continuous learning mindset is constantly throwing off new problems that you like to solve. In fact, when they collaborate on a well-scoped project, Explorers and Strivers do not find it hard to develop mutual respect.

Artisans Versus Givers

Shows up as: Individual mastery of the craft versus collaboration. Artisans are the least team-oriented archetype, and Givers the most. To Givers, Artisans look uncooperative. To Artisans, Givers look like a distraction from their focus on getting the best possible work done.

Steps to mitigate: Givers, you will often need to compromise your expectations when it comes to the way Artisans collaborate. If you can demonstrate how their mastery actually contributes to team success, you will start to bridge the gap, but for the most part, defining your role as helping Artisans thrive even if outside the team may be your best path.

Explorers Versus Givers

Shows up as: Innovation versus helping others thrive. The Giver's desire to maintain team harmony and create positive experiences for all can be at odds with the Explorer's need to try new ways of working and learning. Explorers think Givers hold back experimentation. Givers think Explorers do not care enough about team stability or morale.

Steps to mitigate: Explorers, invite Givers in to your brainstorming and ideation sessions so they are exposed early and can start to consider team implications of business changes. Also, sell your ideas to the team broadly. As that gradually creates buy-in, Givers will work with the energy from emerging agreement.

Archetype Alliances

Just as we can understand conflicts, so can we understand when archetype pairs result in highly positive collaboration. There are four pairs in particular who seem to be natural allies.

You will notice that one of these pairs (Strivers and Pioneers) is *also* a pair that we have just called out in the list of common conflicts. This is not a mistake. Chapter 7 describes how each archetype has its "confident" version, when work is flowing well, and its "fearful" version, when nothing at work is going right. Both versions exist inside each of us and create the potential for the same pair to team well or to be in conflict.

Operators and Givers

These two are both at heart motivated by relationships. They both value teamwork highly and enjoy having friends at work. The Giver's dedication to helping others thrive lines up with the Operator's need for a supportive work environment that allows them to do a good job and then get out to pursue the activities that give their lives meaning. They both value consistency: a well-organized and cohesive workplace.

Pioneers and Explorers

These two are both change-seekers, albeit with different motivations, but the shared comfort with change and pursuit of the new makes them a pair that can spark ideas and channel them into initiatives for their firms.

Strivers and Pioneers

These two are about achievement at work, although their definitions of achievement differ. The Pioneer is often stretching to change the world in some way, small or big, and if their vision turns into firm strategy, then the Striver is the perfect foil to take the vision and turn it into milestones and metrics that they will be happy to push toward.

Artisans and Operators

Artisans generally want to be left alone to develop expertise that they proudly share with the team. Operators can provide the kind of stable environment Artisans need to let them focus on their craft. Meanwhile, the high-quality Artisan work supports the structure and processes that the Operator flourishes in.

■ ■ ■

The next chapter includes stories intended to illustrate the interplay between archetypes on working teams. I have said earlier, I do not believe the archetypes should be used as a recruiting tool. On your teams, you have the mix of profiles that you have. Success at work – for you and your firm – is about helping those profiles work together in pursuit of business objectives and personal fulfillment.

Chapter 3

Putting Archetypes to Work

Over the last several years, I have shared the idea of archetypes at firms around the world, in a wide range of industries: shipping and logistics, telecommunications, private equity, venture capital, healthcare, food, beverages, personal care, retail, e-commerce, apparel, information technology, retail banking, insurance, ride-hailing, delivery services, online payments, hotels, publishing, agricultural chemicals, transportation, automotive, high-tech manufacturing, energy generation, and distribution. I have met with government ministries in multiple countries and nonprofit organizations serving their communities.

No matter the industry, I meet leaders at these events who say they aspire to more personalization in what they offer their workers. When you look at what they are experimenting with, it settles down into four types of change.

First are *flexible work options*, which create more freedom about where and when work can be done and about actual hours worked. You will find programs like these in companies such as Salesforce, Microsoft, SAP in Europe, DBS Bank in Singapore, Banco Santander and Falabella in Latin America, Emirates Group in the UAE, and Toyota in Japan.

Second are *flexible benefits*. Firms offer a range of benefits, including health and wellness options (which are covered in more detail in Chapter 5), financial planning services, additional personal leave, and more. Although there are constraints, employees choose the combination that suits them most at a given time. Examples include Unilever, Google, Vodafone, Wipro in India, Samsung in South Korea, and Natura & Co in Brazil.

Related to this, there have also been experiments to take a flexible approach to total compensation, including base pay, benefits, and, when relevant, even equity. Shopify's Flex Comp is a shining example of what can be offered when the desire to give employees agency in their reward choices overwhelms the many practical difficulties of actually doing it.

Third is *flexible career-pathing*. Grupo Bimbo in Mexico, Alibaba in China, GoTo in Indonesia, Emaar Properties in Dubai, and PwC are among the firms that offer personalized career development programs and internal mobility options, allowing workers to explore different opportunities within the company. In some cases, these programs truly enable individuals to define and redefine the entire direction of their career. In other cases, they can seem more like sophisticated, digitized learning and development programs, using technology (augmented reality [AR]/virtual reality [VR], gamification); micro-learning approaches with short, frequent employee-selected training nuggets (Unilever calls this *snackable learning*, which perfectly captures the idea); and "smart" learning, where AI tools recommend tailored trainings.

These are all good developments and certainly more customized than the old norm, one-size-for-all approach that assumed everyone was trying to progress in the same ways, with the same motivations. Still, the implementation of flexible career pathing has a long way to go on the intimacy side of the "scale plus intimacy" equation.

Fourth is the *flexibility to spend work time on side projects*. This idea has a storied history dating back to World War II when leaders at 3M Company created a program for 15% of their engineers' time to be spent on innovation ideas outside their mainstream jobs. Google imitated the 3M approach in its early years, with a 20% time allocation allowed for personal passion projects.

Blue-collar and manual workers are also included in many firms' plans to increase personalization. The nature of their work makes some of the changes introduced for white-collar workers hard to replicate. At its simplest, there are two areas of change. One is in a flexible approach to shift schedules. Firms around the world – for example, Toyota, Huawei, BYD, Siemens, Proctor & Gamble, Walmart, Caterpillar, Ford, Tata Steel, and AP Moller-Maersk – have all embedded flexibility into what used to be the most rigid, time-bound part of their business systems. The other is the extension of benefits originally designed with white-collar workers in mind – time-off policies, mental and physical health and wellness programs, assessments of workplace comfort, family support and counseling services, and financial counseling are all now more frequently available to their blue-collar colleagues.

In general, true personalization has been hard. The HRMSs were built to standardize and to capture the scale benefits of a single system in use for everyone. The core steps of the talent management journey often look more or less the same for everyone outside the executive ranks.

Starting with the Data About Your Team

No matter the sector, the question I hear with most consistency is, how do we get started?

The simplest first step is to run the quantitative research across your organization. This has two benefits. It allows people to discover their archetype and learn more about themselves. And it gives the project leaders a full picture of the archetype mix of their firm together with a host of related information such as how the archetypes vary by gender, by age, by ethnicity, by country (for multicountry firms), by job type, or by tenure.

The analysis of the survey data will reveal how job attributes are scored and ranked and how that varies for each worker cohort. The values of workers, sources of job satisfaction, job stress, energy, and the intention to stay in a job also all become transparent.

Personal data disclosure legislation varies from country to country, and this first step may need to be run anonymously. The immediate follow-up is to gather workers together for small focus groups, and having tried this several different ways, it is best to gather these groups according to archetype. This will require multiple groups for each archetype, and we have found it useful to build the groups by tenure: a Striver with one year of tenure is often experiencing different positives and negatives than a Striver with 15 years at the firm.

In the focus groups, facilitators will usually start by asking the group what it feels like to be [Archetype X] working at their firm. I have seen this simple question open up lengthy, emotional discussions about positive and negative aspects of work. Armed with new insights about their own archetype, workers are better equipped to understand their experience. Follow-on questions typically include:

- What motivates you at work?
- How do you feel about aspects of our talent management system (e.g. recruiting, training, performance evaluation, compensation, etc.)?
- What is working well on your teams? What is not?

When you aggregate the results of the quantitative research with the focus groups by archetype, you have a rich set of data that no amount of annual engagement surveys could match.

At a global services firm, they learned that the mix of Strivers was almost 2.5 times the norm, 48% compared to the 21% global average. This insight alone caused the firm to reverse course on some people management policies. For example, in response to feedback that the system lacked equity, they had recently eliminated a "faster track" promotion path for high performers after three years. Knowing how much Strivers, particularly younger Strivers, value the recognition and rewards of promotions, they reinstated the faster track option.

A second change emerged from archetype insights. Like so many firms, they were engaged on a multiyear journey to add digital talent into the business, including data architects, data scientists, software engineers, DevOps, and product managers. This demanded not just recruiting from new talent pools but also wrestling with how to integrate the new talent to make them productive and successful.

The typical archetype of the new talent turned out to be different from the other team members. Their Striver mix was much lower. Their Pioneer mix was much higher: 33% compared to 20%. Their Explorer mix was much higher too: 21% compared to 9%.

The focus groups further illustrated the differences. In answer to the question "What motivates you at work?," Strivers would answer with comments like "external recognition," "material success and recognition," "appearing successful," "personal growth," and "getting active feedback on my performance."

Pioneers and Explorers, on the other hand, gave answers such as "learning and trying new things," "absorbing new ways of working," and "innovating for great value."

Quizzed about the firm's existing talent management policies, the answers diverged. Strivers were generally happy. "The performance evaluation system motivates me a lot. It is helpful when my supervisors write a performance review in a very detailed way and lets me know where to improve. It gives me a clear roadmap about where I perform well and how I could improve."

Strivers also want the chance to be seen to be doing well. Some expressed frustration about the termination of the fast track promotion path: "I'm willing to work late, and I don't care so much about work-life balance right now. But it lowers my motivation if I get promoted at the same pace as everyone else, no matter how well I am doing."

Meanwhile, the Pioneers and Explorers in the new talent cohorts were much less comfortable with the performance evaluation system: "I heard that if you want to get a top performance score, you need to work on a very intense project with very long hours. What I really want to do is work on something that's interesting to me—do I have to give up the chance for a top score?"

As a result of the research, this firm has made changes to policies and processes for the new talent. While continuing to reflect firm values and skill-building aspirations, the performance management tool for them is now different than the one used for the other frontline workers, allowing for more evaluation of, and recognition for, the job attributes that Pioneers and Explorers value most highly.

A third insight emerged from studying the group of workers at this firm who support the front line: the middle and back-office teams working, for example, in legal, finance, human resources, technical support, and administrative roles.

Their archetype mix was still weighted to Strivers. But what jumped out was the remarkably high mix of Givers in this group: 30% compared to the firm average of 11%, and even higher for more senior team members.

The focus groups reinforced the special features of this cohort. Givers talk about the motivation that comes from "having a great working relationship with people," "making a positive impact on people around me and on myself," "investing in people growth."

This group was also at the intersection point between the new talent and the other frontline workers and could see all the challenges:

- "Our training content is outdated; it doesn't address the needs of the new talent. I had to abandon 80% of the training material and re-design it myself."

- "Our performance review system is weighted in favor of those working on solving our customer's problems. We need to recognize people for being culture carriers internally and make everyone realize this is something we value."

This distinctively Giver-ish perspective is almost ideal for the roles they are playing, but the firm was running the risk of undervaluing their contributions. Simple changes in recognition programs and in the way leaders talked about these roles, and the people in them, have resulted in higher levels of employee advocacy in this cohort.

This firm was learning the lesson that we have seen at many organizations around the world: the talent management infrastructure and systems are usually designed around one archetype (in their case, it was the Striver). This may reach back to the founders or to seminal events at the center of the culture, or it may simply be the old norm assumptions about who people are at work and how they want to be managed.

Think about your own firm. Which archetype has the talent management system been primarily designed for? At the firms I work with, I make notes on which profiles are being hired, who is getting promoted, and who are the success stories that leaders show to the rest of the organization at public moments (implicitly messaging ". . . be more like this person, and you will succeed here too"). You can quickly make a guess about your own firm, and you'll probably be right. Now, think about all the people who are not that archetype, and ask yourself how the talent system is working for them.

As one focus group participant at the services firm put it, after considering all the research and her own situation, "I'm a Pioneer living in a Striver's world. I just have to get comfortable with that."

Training Team Leaders

Archetype training for leaders – anyone at any level of your organization who is leading a team, from executives to the front line – is a prerequisite for productive use of the tool.

As you will see later, certain archetypes are more often found in executive leadership roles. But throughout the organization, there are teams composed of, and led by, many different archetypes, each with their own ideas about high performance.

Consider this example of a consumer products firm.

Amy is a team leader, a strong performer ascending the higher ranks of middle management, and a Striver. She has worked hard to create opportunities for herself, earned promotions, and enjoyed recognition along the way. For one of her promotions, it came down to her and one other candidate: she crushed it, massively outworking and outperforming the potential rival during the run-up to the decision. She is 41 years old and has her sights set on more senior leadership roles.

On the team she leads are two Operators, one Artisan, one Giver, and another Striver. The youngest member is 27 years old (that's an Operator); the oldest is 58 (that's the Artisan). Their current mission is a turnaround plan for a product that is performing poorly against competitors in a channel where it should be doing better. The skills of the team members have been carefully selected and include consumer insight and market intelligence, pricing, advertising and promotion, supply chain, and finance. Amy is from marketing.

Amy sets up review meetings with the sponsor of the project, who is responsible for all the products sold in this important channel, where the product is struggling. In her mind, this project could be the difference between her next promotion coming six months from now or having to wait a year or more. Success will reflect well on the whole team, especially on her.

At the start of the project, Amy gathered her team for a group discussion about archetypes and their implications for their working style. One of the Operators asked if he could leave work a little early every Tuesday and Thursday, as those were his days to pick up the children from school and take care of them for the evening (his partner covered the other days). After some discussion, Amy suggested he work a little longer on other days of the week (from home if preferable). He agreed.

The Giver offered to organize training in a couple of skill areas, one of which was building a successful cross-functional team. Amy was initially concerned these would take too much time away from delivering the project, and she asked him to keep the trainings as short as they could be while still being helpful.

He also wanted to arrange team events every two weeks, where they could get to know each other better. Everyone agreed to this, except the Artisan. He was older and worked out of a different office than the rest of the team. In fact, he mostly worked remotely and focused on the complex pricing analysis that he had been mastering for years. He said he was concerned about spending too much time traveling for training and for social events – the rest of the team asked him to join the trainings remotely, and the Giver promised to design them so that could work. They gave him a pass for the social get-togethers, after he committed to one team event at the end of the project.

The other Striver on the team was Ajay from finance. He was the same age as Amy and by title, the same job grade. He had joined the firm six months ago from a competitor and was building a reputation as a good contributor. This cross-functional project was his first assignment outside the finance function. Having checked with him in advance, Amy asked the team if they were okay with Ajay leading the meetings she was unable to attend. She explained she did not think there would be many because she was committed to the project, but when it did happen, she needed to know someone would take the lead and keep everything moving along. The rest of the team had no objections.

Each team member had an awareness of, and a language to describe, how their worker archetype influences working styles and choices. Through her training, Amy knows that she tends to dial up pressure on her teams as deadlines approach, in ways that others can find transactional. Her understanding of how other archetypes are motivated puts her in a strong position to adjust her own behavior.

The mission of the team remains paramount. The skills *and* mindsets of the team are the building blocks for success. No one's motivations are unconsciously ignored. They *might* be consciously ignored: several times on the days he was supposed to be with the children Amy had to ask the Operator to work late – but she knew the cost of what she was asking. Done right, this trainable awareness builds a high trust team.

Older Worker Archetypes

A global conglomerate, with businesses in developed and developing markets, was aware of the changing age profile in its workforce of several hundred thousand. After an initial round of archetype research and focus groups with workers over 50 years old in all job types, the leadership team wants to take a few simple steps to get started and to learn what would have the most impact on retention and productivity of the older workers.

The CHRO assembled a consciously multigenerational project team and tasked them to pick two or three initiatives and design key performance indicators (KPIs) that would give an honest view of value and progress.

The team was mindful of country differences. In their European markets, for example, the combined Pioneer and Striver mix shrank enormously (by a half or even two-thirds) in the 55+ years old cohort, and interesting work became the most important job attribute (discussed in more detail in Chapter 6). Whereas in Indonesia, a critical market for the firm, the archetype mix changes only slightly with age, and older workers (like younger ones) rated good compensation as most important.

They shortlisted six ideas:

- Launch a *reverse mentoring* program in which younger workers coach older workers (the reality of this is often more two-way than one way, but the idea is still valuable).

- Start an affinity group for older workers.

- Start several age-defined affinity groups, starting with older workers and Gen Z.

- Design and pilot a new training program specifically for older workers in two of their divisions and recruit older workers as trainers.

- Create phased retirement options, catering to the motivations and skills of their older workers, starting with a step down to a three-day week from full-time.

- Design a *return to work* program, initially with a part-time option mainly focused on mentoring and coaching, a direct appeal to the high mix of Artisans and Givers in their older worker cohort.

At an early review, someone referred to the *Grandternity* leave program that Cisco had created – paid time off for a new grandchild's arrival. It was immediately added to the shortlist as an example of meeting your older workers where they are, in this case looking for flexibility exactly when they need it (the number-one ask that workers make of their firms in support of wellness).

They will end up prioritizing phased retirement options in developed markets and affinity groups in developing markets.

The team's assessment is that all of these programs have value: it is now a question of investment appetite and timing.

Archetypes tell us that workers have distinct motivations. But if surveying all of your workers and keeping a record of their archetype is too hard to do or violates data privacy principles in certain markets, people leaders can still make progress without knowing every single person's archetype. They just need to know that certain archetypes will be most positively impacted by certain programs.

Consider the packages that mobile phone operators offer. They do not need to know every customer's personal preferences. They simply need to know that there is a segment of customers who particularly value unlimited data. Another segment with teenage children wants a family plan. Another segment of frequent travelers wants international call minutes and the least expensive international roaming. Another segment of heavy content and entertainment users wants as much free or discounted streaming of music, subscription video, or sports content they can possibly get. If they design packages around the right sets of features and market them effectively, the customers most motivated by those features will be attracted to the best package for them.

The New Tools

Generative AI tools are accelerating at the same time as our appreciation that workers are heterogenous in their motivations. Millions of white-collar jobs may be impacted by GenAI. Some will be automated away. Some will be augmented. And countless new jobs will be created, both to create the technology but mostly to use it in a myriad of new applications.

Putting Archetypes to Work

In the world of human resource management itself, early runner insurgent firms are deploying GenAI-based solutions across a range of talent use cases. SeekOut, Fuel50, eightfold. ai, Talentware, and Reejig are a few of many firms now using deep-learning AI as assistants for employees looking to manage their careers, for employers looking to get the right people into the right jobs, and for recruiters looking to improve talent acquisition, from creating a job description all the way to initial contact with a qualified candidate.

Some of these new solutions will fade without trace, but some are going to be breakout successes, creating new value for individuals and for firms. Properly deployed, this technology can enable us to de-average the workforce in ways that CHROs want.

Firms have deployed self-service career management platforms as part of their HRMS. Employees log on to see what job opportunities there might be inside the firm for people with their skills at their level. The next generation of these platforms can improve the odds that people are well matched to opportunities. That serves everyone's interests. The improvements can come from two sources:

- First, *more information*. The new models are trying to integrate data from internal firm records (for example, resumes submitted with job applications, organization charts) with external information from networking sites such as LinkedIn or GitHub, which can often be richer sources. Firms can be surprised how little they actually know about their employees. One contemporary example: some firms have no idea how many of their workers also have gig economy jobs. The workers may prefer to conceal it, and the firms do not have a mechanism to ask. I suspect this was part of the reason for the brilliant "U-Work" program at Unilever, which allows their employees to have second jobs transparently. This program dignifies gig work at a time when some mid- and lower-paid workers around the world need to boost their income.

- Second, *better matching algorithms*. This is where well-trained artificial intelligence can improve or accelerate performance. The current paradigm for matching is skills based. The skills of the individual are compared to the skill requirements of the role, and a compatibility assessment is generated. Those skills can be technical, managerial, and even, although rarely, behavioral. Career path options can be generated, specific skill developments recommended, and in theory the recommendations balance the needs of the firm with the best interests of the individual.

We know that skills are only one part of success in a job. There is a common point of view that the half-life of skills has fallen to an average of around five years, and just two to three years for ones that are technology-based. Skills can be improved and new ones learned when workers have a mindset for re-skilling. Archetypes are a powerful way for us to understand those mindsets.

Imagine that motivations and archetypes were folded into these matching algorithms, as another component predicting an individual's fit with a role. This will elevate the effectiveness of the algorithm by understanding instances where skills fit but mindset and motivations do not (the experience we observe when we say that so-and-so is talented but "just in the wrong role") and likewise decoding matches where motivations fit well even if skills need to be further developed.

Who Was Your Talent System Built For?

Firms unconsciously or subconsciously design their talent systems around a dominant archetype. For firms more than about 40 years old, this is often the Striver, because the core values of the Striver emerge from the professional management model that came to dominate organizational thinking during the early twentieth century. For younger firms, particularly ones with founders still involved, the central archetype might be the Pioneer, although almost by definition it can be hard to build systems and processes that suit Pioneers because they will often want to tear them down and build something new. Even founder-led firms borrow parts of the Striver playbook for talent management.

The talent norms of successful younger firms include more role flexibility, plenty of Super Individual Contributors (Super ICs), a focus on apprenticeship (the super ICs are often involved as masters coaching apprentices), cross-functional teams everywhere (like the one Amy was leading), and an appreciation of the journey of each individual's career (for which you need the career passport I describe in Chapter 6) as much as for titles.

Knowing the archetype you have, and the archetype your talent system is most adapted to, unlocks the ability to make the changes required for your firm to be a place with good jobs for all the archetypes on your team.

I joined a "Top 200" event with a Nordic-based international transportation company, an ambitious firm committed to the idea that being a great place to work is the precondition for its people to thrive and perform at the top of their potential. I listened eagerly to the CHRO describe the three-point plan: be a safe place to work, be an inclusive place to work, and be a place with truly engaging leaders.

The first two points of the plan are clear, simple, and measurable. The third seemed more complex to me. What I had completely failed to understand was the archetype composition of the leadership team. When we gathered the data, there was, as I could predict, a high mix of Pioneers in this top leader group. What I did not expect was that the second most common leader archetype was Givers, at 21% – much higher than the general Nordic working population and extremely high by the standards of the other leadership teams I have spent time with. I understood then that the third ambition – to have engaging leaders supporting their colleagues to be their best – was powerfully realistic. Because that is exactly how Givers are motivated.

Happy Work, Happy Life? Lessons from the Nordics

Let us linger a little longer in the Nordics: there may be more to learn. They are famously "happy" societies, routinely making the top 10 in the World Happiness Index each year (Finland has been first for the last seven years).[1]

We ran our research in Denmark, Sweden, Norway, and Finland. These countries have many things in common, including high living standards and strong welfare systems, but each is unique. The archetype mix was similar across the four with one exception in Finland,[2] where the mix of Artisans was the highest we have seen anywhere around the world.

Happiness is certainly not the same as job satisfaction, but they may be relatives. When you spend time with firms in the

Nordics, it is clear that their working norms have evolved in ways that address the stressors and energy sources described in Chapter 5.

People stress about workload and long hours. In Norway, Finland, and Sweden, the standard work week is 40 hours; in Denmark, it's 37. This is 10–15% lower than the United States. Mandatory vacation for full-time workers is 25 days per year, but what most firms offer is 30 days, and 35 is not unknown. The United States norm is 10 days for new workers, rising to 15 days for longer-tenured employees (and there is some data to suggest Americans do not always take all their vacation days).[3]

Our research says flexible work hours, time off, and leave-of-absence policies are among the best things firms can offer to support wellness at work. In Finland, workers have the right to move their start and finish times at work by up to three hours outside their employer's norm. Stress-related leaves of absence are treated more or less the same as leaves for other medical conditions. Denmark's "flexicurity" labor model guarantees easy mobility between jobs and a generous income safety net for the unemployment period.[4] Norway and Sweden have among the most generous paid maternity leave programs; Finland is top five globally for paid paternity.

These are the enabling laws and customs. Chapter 2 noted how unusual the workers in three of these four Nordic countries are, in their ranking of interesting work as the most important job attribute, ahead of good compensation. When we study Nordic women and men separately, we find that for women, good relationships are about as important (sometimes more so) as interesting work. Finns, with that heavy population of Artisans, are less focused on good relationships. At the same time, the Pioneer mix is low across the board, so some of the conflicts I describe later – between executives and the front line – are less visible. The archetype mix is well adjusted for the flatter, more collaborative style of organization that I have worked with in these markets.

None of this is accidental. Social and cultural norms have converged to decide that work-life balance is the objective. The systems are delivering with sustained success. It does come at a cost: personal income tax rates in these countries are high. And it would not suit every culture. Elsewhere the objectives are different. The long hours, the missed vacation days, the conflicts at work – elsewhere, the underlying assumption may be that those are all worth it if it helps you build the next Apple, the next Tesla, the next BYD, the next ByteDance, the next OpenAI.

It's a brave new world in human resource management. For one thing, it's often not called "Human Resources" anymore, but People Operations, People Systems, Employee Experience, or People Experience. Name changes are the outward and visible sign of an inward shuffling of the feet. We are alive at last to the idea that there is no further need to assume there is an average worker for whom an averaged-out talent system will do more or less fine.

Innovation, product, sales, and marketing teams long ago moved on from the scale-driven, mass-market view of customers to nuanced ideas about segments and even unit-of-one products and solutions. Talent teams can now aspire to the same for their workers. They can embrace the rich diversity of motivations as an asset, use the new insights to help a wider diversity of people reach full potential, and drive business results through more satisfied, engaged individuals on higher performing teams.

Putting Archetypes to Work

Chapter 4

Leaders

L eaders are intensively observed, dissected, and discussed. They have an outsized impact on the lives of the people in their organization. What are their motivations at work? When we understand a leader's archetype, there is a good chance we can not only help them develop in their leadership role but also improve their interactions with others who may not be motivated by the same factors.

I review our research on leaders later in the chapter. First, two stories about historical figures who epitomize some of the most commonly observed leader motivations.

Alfred Sloan, Striver as Leader

Alfred Sloan defined a model of leadership that still feels very familiar.

The success of General Motors I described earlier emerged from a starting point in the earliest part of the twentieth century, which was chaotic and uncertain. The automotive boom created several hundred firms in the United States, of which in the end only three survived. We are currently living through an electric vehicle version of the same story.

This is what happens when vast new markets are created: many species are attracted to the profit pool. Most perish, unable to combine product, business model, and economics in ways that customers and investors will support. A few survive and flourish.

Imagine the excitement in the first decades of the twentieth century, as car firms formed, merged, restarted, and went bankrupt, each pushing boundaries in this new industry of personal transportation. In 1908, two important moments occurred: Henry Ford launched the Model T, and William C. Durant created General Motors Corporation out of a group of car and parts companies he had been assembling over the previous few years.

Billy Durant's life was a roller coaster of business wins and fails. He was a high school dropout who made his first fortune building the leading manufacturer of horse-drawn vehicles.

There is a worn-out old quip – attributed to Henry Ford although it's unclear he ever said it – that goes like this: "If I had asked them what they wanted, they would have said faster horses."

This was not, evidently, the Durant point of view. Moving from horse-drawn carriages into automobiles seemed to him a one-step move; he took it swiftly and went all in. A serial acquirer over his entire business career, in 1904 he took control of Buick Motors and over the next few years acquired around a dozen fledgling car companies and another 10 parts and accessories companies, which he integrated into one group.

Overleveraged from all those deals, Billy Durant lost control of General Motors in 1910 (exactly the kind of mistake that Sloan will tut-tut him for later). Five years later, he regained control via his ownership of shares in Chevrolet, which became a part of the GM family. More acquisitions followed, notably of the Hyatt Roller Bearing Company of Newark, New Jersey, where Sloan was in charge.

Hyatt manufactured anti-friction bearings for rear axles and transmissions. Sloan had built relationships with Ford and most of the other auto entrepreneurs since taking control of the company in 1905 when its original founder was ousted (one more example of the creative destruction that is part of the industry's origins story).

Now Sloan was part of the General Motors family, and he rapidly became president of United Motors, the unit that owned the parts and accessories companies Durant had been steadily acquiring.

A self-aware Durant – I do not know if he was self-aware, only that he had a short attention span and was always on to the next shiny thing – might have seen in Sloan exactly what he needed. There is a long history of creative founders pairing up with commercial managers to bring their dreams to life. Bill Bowerman of Nike needed Phil Knight. Calvin Klein needed Barry Schwartz. Howard Schultz at Starbucks needed Orin Smith. Steve Jobs needed Tim Cook.

This was not to be at GM. It took almost no time for Sloan to come to his conclusion about Durant. In his book, he is curt about the founder – "Basic business administration was not his strength"[1] – but he did not progress his thinking to the idea that with the two of them working together, the combination of strengths could be a winning formula.

You can hear the clenched teeth in that assessment. Just as Frederick Taylor found the idea of worker's soldiering to be incomprehensible and offensive, Sloan had a powerfully negative reaction to Durant's style. He could not tolerate the lack of controls. His first act of restructuring was to create a central Appropriations Committee, which he chaired, in an attempt to rein in the car divisions, which all argued for more investment, all missed their capital budget targets, and all believed that they, and only they, should be forgiven for doing so.

The entirety of Sloan's career from this point on is the story of his constantly evolving efforts to create the systems and controls needed to manage a complex, growing enterprise without stifling the entrepreneurs who make the products and serve the customers.

In the short term, a market crisis and an internal crisis combined to change the leadership team at GM for good. Demand for cars crashed in the autumn of 1920. Ford reduced prices by almost 30%; GM was left with stranded inventory and collapsing revenue. The market collapse led to a stock price collapse, and Durant, caught in a short squeeze perhaps or in some other ways fatally compromised in his shareholding position, resigned. GM was on the edge of bankruptcy.

A consortium of banks and the DuPont company took the majority of Durant's shares in a balance sheet restructuring. Pierre DuPont was appointed president and joined the newly created, four-person Executive Committee, which Sloan chaired.

Sloan had been working on a new organizational model even before the crisis. In another teeth-sucking aside, he describes showing his draft organization plan to Durant in late 1919. Durant, he says, "appeared to accept it favorably, though he did nothing about it."[2]

His organizational plan, eventually adopted as official corporate policy, was founded on two principles. They are short:

- "The responsibility attached to the chief executive of each operation shall in no way be limited. Each such organization headed by its chief executive shall be complete in every necessary function and enabled to exercise its full initiative and logical development.

- Certain central organization functions are absolutely essential to the logical development and proper control of the Corporation's activities."[3]

There it is. The units should not be constrained from doing what they want, but then again there should be some shared things, which only the Center can do. This is the essential challenge of all multicountry, multiproduct, or multi-anything firms. What should the units that are closest to customers do? What should the Center do? How to coordinate between them? What style of leadership will work best?

Sloan confronted these questions, had a solution, implemented the solution, and made of it a gigantic global success that many others have copied.

This is about more than just organizational design, though. Much of the commentary gets this wrong. This is what he goes on to say: "Every enterprise needs a concept of its industry. There is a logical way of doing business in accordance with the facts and circumstances of an industry, if you can figure it out."[4]

Exactly right. This is what we would call strategy (Sloan prefers the term *policy*), and the only way to understand Sloan's success at GM is as the outcome of a set of strategy choices supported by – and fully integrated with – an organizational design and a people plan that could deliver the outcomes and that could evolve as strategies changed.

Ford, in Sloan's view, had a static concept of the industry, where low price points dominated and where, with only two cars (the Model T, high volume, low price; and the Lincoln, low volume, high price), it controlled more than half the market.

In 1920 GM had no concept of the industry. It produced seven different product lines, but only two of them (the Buick and Cadillac) had coherent ideas about their customers. Between these two and the other five brands, there was price confusion, consumer overlap, and cannibalization.

As I described in Chapter 1, Sloan's solution was the "anti-Ford" concept. GM would make six car models. The price steps between each line would not be too large, and there would be no overlaps in the price bands. At the bottom end, GM would finally go after Ford, using its Chevrolet brand to attack the Model T; at the top end, the Cadillac brand would target anything slightly below "fancy priced" cars.

This radical idea was underpinned by Sloan's conviction that the industry was on the verge of a transition that GM could help to accelerate. In hindsight, he saw three phases: the early years before 1908, when cars were prohibitively expensive; 1908 to mid-1920s, when cars became a mass-market item and Ford ruled; and finally, post the mid-1920s, when the market began to stratify.

How much of this transition was predestined, and how much was the result of GM's own actions? We end up asking this question about all pivotal technologies: were ubiquitous smartphones inevitable, or was it only thanks to Steve Jobs and Apple?

There were four things going on in the car industry at this time that contribute to the transition.

First, installment selling. Sloan had established the General Motors Acceptance Corporation (GMAC) back in 1919 as a source of funding for consumers and for dealers. By 1925, 65% of new cars on the roads of America had been financed in some way.

Second, the trading of cars was by the mid-1920s an established custom that was unthinkable just 10 years earlier.

Third, closed body designs shot up from 10% of cars sold in 1919 to 65% in 1925, opening up car use to vastly more people in more climate zones.

Fourth, most intriguing, and most radical, was the concept of the "annual model," the idea that an American family, enjoying rising income, could reasonably expect to trade up their car every year or two, so the car companies had to produce new versions, or entirely new models, and release them yearly to capture consumer attention.

These evolutions crippled Ford. The Model T's open body design started to look antiquated. The complete lack of consumer choice ("any color so long as it's black") compared poorly to six car brands over at GM starting to produce new models every year. Ford's loss of market share was precipitous. He closed his flagship River Rouge plant in 1927 and spent an entire year retooling it for new models, leaving the low price tier wide open for Chevrolet. Sloan says, "Mr. Ford, who had had so many brilliant insights in earlier years, seemed never to understand how completely the market had changed from the one in which he had made his name and to which he was accustomed."[5]

It was no longer "basic transportation" that Americans needed from a new car. They could get basic transportation from a used car. For their second or third new car, they wanted something more: more comfort, more convenience, more power, more style. The procession of GM cars in their line-up offered plenty of options.

This is the lesson of these transitions: a firm's strengths from the prior era are often the very things that will prevent success from continuing in the new era. Transitions are mass extinctions, as firms work to establish the new rules for competition. Ford survived its near-death experience in the mid-1920s but before long surrendered overall market leadership to GM and has not regained it in the 100 years since.

It's easy to underestimate the complexity of Sloan's integration of organizational design and financial control systems. Today, all firms of any meaningful size have financial controls that look something like the ones he created, adapted for their own situations and industries. He was creating as he went along, constantly tweaking and forever in a dialogue with the divisions and staff teams about their roles, their goals, and their metrics.

This is exactly what he judged Durant to be so incompetent at – but in fairness, *no one* had ever designed a system like the one Sloan created, and it's far more than "basic business administration." As the chapters of his book flow on, we can watch the creation of the world's first modern multinational company, decision by decision, committee by committee.

He never wavered from his belief that what he called "coordinated decentralization" was the key to unlock organizational performance. You must have in place the right motivators (in the form of incentives and systems that reflect the motivations of different workers) and the right opportunities (in the form of decentralized decision-making and accountability). A steady flow of operating data makes coordinated decentralization work.

We can look at the system Sloan conceived and created as many steps on from Taylor's scientific management but emerging from similar origins. They both cared deeply about efficiency: for Taylor, maximum efficiency means maximum prosperity. To achieve it, he wanted to eliminate variability through systematic and continuous process improvement.

For Sloan, too, efficiency was the driver of success. Efficiency goes hand in hand with scale: if you attack scale, he said, you damage efficiency.

Sloan operated on a vastly bigger canvas than Taylor, conceiving early on of a large, diversified company. He never thought the goal was to eliminate variability: rather, it was to build a system that could allow variability to exist, to allow innovation to occur, to encourage disruptions – and to do all that without the wheels falling off, through the combination of financial controls and "controlled decentralization."

In this conception of what a company could be, he single-handedly led the world into a new era of business, the era of professional management.

The professionalization of management enabled a new generation of companies to scale and sustain themselves beyond the vision of their founders. At its best, this system drove astonishing levels of innovation, growth, and value with its combinations of standards, routines, and predictability. Professional management routines underpin business success stories from McDonald's to Ikea to Southwest Airlines. For the first time, management became a career path for millions of workers, separate from both capital and labor.

All of this descends directly from Alfred Sloan.

I have argued earlier in this book that changes in firm strategies, sources of advantage, the prevalence of networks and ecosystems, the impact of artificial intelligence, and the changing career demands of workers are all combining today to nudge the professional manager out of the spotlight at the center of the organization. Firms will need fewer managers, and their roles will be different. Rather than shuffling information, creating routines, and issuing instructions to subordinates, they will spend their time supporting the mission-critical roles: the people who innovate, execute, and work directly to deliver the firm's promise.

In the end, the reason the Alfred Sloans of the business world exist is to nurture and scale the innovations of the Billy Durants.

Francesco Datini, Pioneer as Leader

Sloan epitomizes the Striver leader: a planner, dedicated, loyal, highly focused on results and outcomes, not a risk-taker. Millions of executives have followed his example. In fact, his way became the default way for firms to think about talent. Firms promised job stability, deep generalist management training, a predictable path up the organization, with title bumps and pay increases along the way – and in return expected commitment and productivity.

There is another model of leadership we should keep in view. It's always been there, and in our current era of disruptions, leaps in the capabilities of technology, staggering corporate valuations, and vast private capital pools, not to mention yards of books on how to be one, the entrepreneur as leader stands in contrast to the professional manager.

My exemplar for the entrepreneur leader is a late fourteenth-century Italian called Francesco di Marco Datini. To ground ourselves, the human population of the world in his lifetime was approximately 400 million (compared to just over 8 billion now) and global GDP was approximately US$250 billion (compared to about US$100 trillion).

Datini was a Tuscan born around 1335. Over the course of his long life (he lived to be 75), he built a successful trading firm that brought him tremendous wealth.

We would probably call his firm a *mid-cap* – Datini's business never reached the scale and prestige of the great international trading houses of his era – the Soderini or the Guinigi, bankers and merchants to the popes – but he was successful, in today's terms certainly a multimillionaire. What is special about Datini is that, thanks to him, we know how an entrepreneur of his era went about day-to-day business.

The reason we know is that, in 1870, around 500 of his account books, 150,000 letters, 300 partnership deeds, and 400 insurance policies were discovered in the stairwell of the mansion in Prato, Italy, that he and his wife occupied for the last decade of his life (a mansion he spent considerable time and money designing and building and that he bequeathed to the city of Prato in his will). It's the single most important archive of business history of the Middle Ages. In 1957, biographer Iris Origo published her study of all the papers in a book called *The Merchant of Prato.*

Origo is an interesting character in her own right. Born in England and educated in Florence, she and her mother moved to Italy after her father died and took up residence in the Villa Medici in Fiesole. Fiesole is not more than 20 miles from Prato.

She knew the places and the people from whom Datini came. I have an image of her in my head – completely imagined – motoring up from her home near Siena to Prato to Bologna to Florence – places Datini had lived and in Prato perhaps stopping for a cappuccino in the Piazza del Comune and staring up at the huge late nineteenth-century statue of her subject, in white Carrara marble, in the middle of the Piazza, before driving home to read a few more of his letters.

Datini's private letters are preserved only from 1372 – they offer sidelong glimpses of what was on the mind of a prosperous entrepreneur. The business correspondence, contracts, and account books start much earlier.

In 1350, at around 15 years old, Datini left Prato and moved to Avignon in Provence in southeastern France. His father, mother, and two of his siblings had died in the Great Plague, leaving him and a brother, Stefano. Avignon was booming. This was the pinnacle of the Avignon Papacy, and the city was the center of trade between Italy and Flanders. Tuscans were the uber traders, and Avignon offered opportunities in wool, cloth, wheat, barley, linen, armor, spices, dyes, silks, oil, leather, fruit, brocades, veils, silverware, and painted panels of gold.

He was obviously talented. By 1358, he was doing well enough in Avignon to summon Stefano to join him. Initially the focus was armor, sourced mainly from Milan, wrapped in straw, packed into bales held together with canvas, and moved on mule-back over the Alps to Avignon.

In 1363 he opened his first shop; by 1367 he had three. Each was opened with a partnership structure. Datini may not have invented the partnership structure as a corporate form, but he certainly advanced its use (and abuse), and there was no business undertaking over his long career that was not a partnership.

Each partner received shares in proportion to the capital they injected or the services they rendered (what we would now call "sweat equity"). If a partner paid in extra sums of money, they earned a fixed rate of interest in the 7–8% range. Capital withdrawals attracted a 20% penalty.

All the partnerships were time-defined, usually two to three years, and in that time no partnership member was allowed to belong to any other partnership and should trade only for his own firm. Datini ignored this provision almost entirely – he formed multiple companies, and he alone belonged to each and controlled management of each. The concept of a holding company (which in effect was what he created and led) came to be fully realized a few decades later, with the Medici.

From armor, he moved swiftly into multiple other categories: he opened a wine tavern and a draper's shop. He went into money changing. He traded salt, saffron, richly embroidered materials for priestly vestments, and religious pictures. On the religious pictures, quality was not necessarily his number-one priority, but he was always customer-focused. In July 1373 he wrote to his supplier in Florence, describing what he needed, "A panel of Our Lady on a background of fine gold, with two doors, and a pedestal with ornaments and leaves......Let there be in the center Our Lord on the Cross, or Our Lady, whichever you find—I do not care so long as the figures are handsome and large. Also, a panel of Our Lady in fine gold, of the same kind, but a little smaller, to cost four florins, but no more."[6]

In 1382 he moved back to Prato. The focus of this period was wool (he joined the powerful Arte della Lana guild in Prato) but four years later moved to Florence and launched the period of his greatest business success.

It was a choppy phase in Florentine history. Many of the great banking houses – the Peruzzi and the Bardi among others – had collapsed from the default on his debt of Edward III, King of England. The banking failures in turn caused trading house failures. Datini writes that living in Florence was to be in daily fear of war, pestilence, famine, and insurrection. He flourished anyway, craftily diversifying and building his midsize multinational.

Tuscan merchants like Datini concentrated on Flanders, Spain, and England, trading wool, cloth, spices, jewels, and works of art. Their supply chain was dependent on Genoese and Venetian galleys sailing from the East, across the Mediterranean and up the Atlantic coast to Flanders. Shipwrecks or pirate attacks introduced volatility into prices. Datini used a number of tactics to manage that risk.

First, he joined the silk merchants guild in Florence and then opened a shop on Via Por Santa Maria, on the northern side of the River Arno, leading right into the famous Ponte Vecchio. With these moves, he installed himself deeply into the Florentine business community.

His main approach to growth, and to risk management, was constant diversification. This is Datini's entrepreneurial genius: like some of today's most successful founders, he was a serial business builder. He was constantly innovating, scaling his innovation, and looking for the next opportunity at the same time. He started out as an armorer and mercer, then moved into cloth-making in Prato, then became a shopkeeper in Florence, then import/export, then into underwriting, and even at one point into banking.

The structure of his firms was very simple and very rigid. At the bottom were the Garzoni, shop boys, office boys, and messengers. Next came the Fattori Scrivani or Fattori Contabili, whose main role was bookkeeping. Double-entry bookkeeping was well established by the middle of the fourteenth century, and Datini used it for all of his ledgers. Then came the Fattori proper. They carried out the instructions of the owners and would be eligible to become managers of foreign branches. They received a salary but no profit share: profits were just for the partners.

His geographic expansion – if you are a late fourteenth-century trader from Prato, going international with your own operations was definitely a big step, in risk and in potential growth – followed the same diversification protocols he had learned in Italy and Avignon.

By 1382 he was established in Pisa, by 1392 in Florence and Genoa, by 1393 in Spain, and by 1394 in the Balearic Islands. Avignon continued to operate throughout.

Datini had a repeatable model for expansion.

First, choose a city where other firms had established trade agreements. Next, pick one of those firms to start to deal with. Then, send one of your own agents to do "on-the-ground" observation of the market. Finally, after a couple of years, form your own company with one of your partners.

There's nothing rash here. The letters show how purposeful he was, willing to invest capital and his own time when he saw an opportunity for more growth. And he was diligent about keeping his nose clean in the communities where he based his firms.

An earlier generation of merchants had conspicuously participated in all aspects of their city's life: trade, industry, banking, politics. This no doubt had advantages, but it also embeds risk. If your politicians lose favor, your business may suffer. Datini avoided politics as much as he could – maybe another factor in his profitable longevity.

He remained apolitical, but he was a religious man. At the top of the page on every Datini great ledger, he wrote the words "In the name of God and profit." This may not stand up to contemporary scrutiny as a mission and purpose statement, but it does offer us clarity on his answer to the question we want to ask all entrepreneurs and founders: why?

Success came at a cost. By his own accounts, Datini worked extraordinarily hard. He was a poor delegator and worked long hours until almost the end of his life. He did not have a glimmer of work-life balance. He slept four hours a night, worked around the clock, and made his teams do the same. In letters to his wife, he describes dreaming about shipwrecks and lost fortunes; and he goes on and on about how difficult business can be.

In the private account books, we learn about his personal expenditure, about family events, and occasionally about his reflections on wider topics. He records his prodigious gift-giving, mainly to friends and to the church. He spent prolifically on clothes, and he especially coveted gowns and cloaks. He owned 10 long gowns (like the one he is wearing in the statue in Prato): five for everyday wear, two with fur linings, two very grand ones for special occasions, and one lined with scarlet taffeta.

No gray tees and plain hoodies here.

Datini returned to Prato in 1401 and spent his last decade in the palazzo he had spent all those years designing and building from afar. It is now the museum home of the documents discovered there.

Much of his story feels very, very ancient. It was 650 years ago. Mules carrying bales of straw across the Alps. The unimaginably slow speed of communication. The vagaries of piracy and bad weather having so much impact on the business. But in other ways his world feels very recognizable.

He was a founder and entrepreneur who was extremely hands-on with the business, sometimes to a fault. There was a well-established organizational design with very few layers. He was highly flexible in moving from one sector to another and from one location to another, in pursuit of the next growth opportunity. He managed risk through diversification. He had a repeatable model for international expansion. His consistent use of partnership structures was a way to manage the balance sheet. His record keeping was exemplary: he knew every detail of every transaction. He was completely focused on his customers and his suppliers: almost all the business letters are to one or other of these.

Origo is a scrupulous biographer, but it is possible sometimes to detect a faint distaste for Datini's slavish dedication to work, the personal sacrifices he makes year in and year out, his seeming misanthropy, occasional avarice, and general distrust of those he worked with. There is a certain grumpiness in some of the letters: the endless complaining asides about how difficult his situation is, how hard he is working, and how much he has to attend to every detail because no one else can be relied on.

Assessments of him have bounced from the critical to the sympathetic over the decades since the publication of her book. From where we sit today in the mid-2020s – in an era that idolizes entrepreneurs, makes a fetish of them, loves a good pivot, admires a founder searching for financing – in our era, Datini is an overlooked role model.

"He was not a model boss or human being, tidily packaged for emulation. Driven by demons, he could drive those around him to fury and despair. His tale is [thus] both instructive and cautionary, filled with lessons about innovation, character, leadership and values,"[7] said Walter Isaacson, and the person he's describing is Steve Jobs. Maybe what Isaacson is saying about Jobs is the same thing Origo is trying to say about Datini: if you are a driven, successful entrepreneur, you do not get to have it all. You give up a lot, because you are all about your business, and the business is all about you.

Datini had a best friend, Ser Lapo Mazzei. He was the protégé of a family acquaintance; he joined Datini as an apprentice and eventually became a partner. Reading their correspondence now is revealing: Ser Lapo is continuously saying, in a nutshell, take a rest, stop working so hard, go home and see your wife. How much more do you need? When is enough enough?

When it's all for God and profit, maybe enough is never enough. He has much in common with founders I meet and study today. They work all the time, they obsess about the talent around them, they worry about money, they sometimes second-guess their business partners, and they sometimes second-guess themselves. But underneath it all, they have an unshakeable belief in what they are doing and in why they have to do it. This is why, whether we like them or not, we find them so compelling.

Datini is the Pioneer's Pioneer. He has the stubbornness and energy to keep going even in the face of impossible difficulties. He is fully at ease changing the rules in pursuit of his goals, and he's quite prepared to "go it alone" if he has to.

What Do Leaders Want from Work?

Let us return from fourteenth-century Europe, via twentieth-century America, to modern times and modern leadership ideas.

If Datini's is the earliest account to show the Pioneer resilience required to succeed as an entrepreneur leader and if Sloan is the architect of the Striver professional manager, it is Jack Welch at General Electric who defined peak professional management.

Welch is much written about but should not get all the credit for his firm's success. His predecessor, Reginald Jones (CEO from 1972 to 1981), created the central strategic planning function, pioneered value analytics, and decentralized GE into 150 strategic business units (SBUs), each with its own profit and loss statement. Jones moved leaders around from one SBU to another, cementing professional management as the transferable skill driving the corporation. Under his leadership, GE excelled: revenues doubled, profits tripled. Jones was one of the most admired executives in the United States, a counselor to presidents.

Welch became CEO in 1981. He saw change coming. There were tough new competitors from Japan and Korea. He also saw future growth opportunities in Asia. And he had a driving competitive ambition to deliver far greater total shareholder returns than Jones had.

In his first few years as CEO he delayered the organization, cutting head count 18% and shrinking the central planning team from 30 down to 8 (the well-known "Neutron Jack" phase: the buildings were left standing but not the people). He redesigned the organization into 15 lines of business organized in three "circles." He closed 25 plants and invested $8B in other ones (much of that investment went on introducing robots, reducing the workforce, and changing assembly line techniques), explicitly to tackle the quality and cost challenges from Japan and Korea. He sold 117 businesses. He designed new incentive systems for leaders, putting 3,000 executives into share option schemes. The subsequent shareholder success during his term as CEO is legendary: revenues up six times, market value up 30 times (although his ability to "manage earnings" using the GE Capital business has recently been much criticized).

The later collapse of GE, first slowly and then very quickly, under Welch's successors, and the eventual re-emergence of a profoundly restructured and smaller business under CEO Larry Culp, demonstrates once again that different eras demand different leadership norms and different talent models.

It was during the Welch era, and increasingly ever since, that advice for leaders has proliferated. A partial, albeit strenuously researched, list of book titles on the subject published in the last 30 years includes *Leadership by Insanity, Leadership by Example, Alpha Leadership, Heroic Leadership, Adaptive Leadership,*

Fierce Leadership, Courageous Leadership, Quirky Leadership, Charismatic Leadership, Timeless Leadership, Slow Leadership, Unnatural Leadership, Champion Leadership, True Leadership, Leadership by Virtue, The Leadership Gap, The Leadership Game, Leadership Jazz, Leadership Secrets, Leadership Matters, Leadership Is an Art, Leadership Is Dead, Leading with Conviction, Leadership Is Not for Cowards, Bootstrap Leadership, Bad Leadership, High Altitude Leadership, The "I" of Leadership, Superstar Leadership, Reasonable Leadership, Life-Changing Leadership, Open Leadership, Reality-based Leadership, Lemon Leadership, Tribal Leadership, Quiet Leadership, Energy Leadership, Organic Leadership, Inclusive Leadership, Remarkable Leadership, Virtual Leadership, Catalytic Leadership, Toy Box Leadership, Servant Leadership, Sacrificial Leadership, Primal Leadership, Legitimate Leadership, Dynamic Leadership, Elegant Leadership, True Leadership, Prophetic Leadership, Naked Leadership, and a personal favorite, *Liquid Leadership,* which I'm sure is a great book but makes me think of what I would need after reading all these.

We have such high expectations of leaders. What do they want at work?

Of course, we recognize that "leaders" are not just in the C-suite. The most critical roles in the organization might not even appear on the typical organization chart, and if they do, they may not be at the top. Brazilian retailer Magazine Luiza celebrates the front line as their heroes. "I know we must continue to be more professional as we grow. That is important," says the company's president, Luiza Helena Trajano, "but I also know that we must keep the store manager as king or queen of the company, with all of us working to serve their needs. We cannot lose focus on who's the real boss: it is our store manager."[8]

Nonetheless, we needed a definition. Our chosen short-hand for leaders in the research is *executives*, who carry titles like chief executive officer, executive vice president, senior vice president, vice president, executive director, owner, or partner. On average across our 19 countries, this group represents roughly 4% of workers. There may be some with executive titles who are not playing what we conventionally think of as leadership roles. Likewise, there are doubtless some leaders who do not carry one of these titles.

The first learning that jumps out is that the proportion of Pioneers is higher among executives than for other workers. This is true in almost all countries. Unafraid to take risks, willing to go it alone if that's what it takes, the Pioneer is highly focused on changing the world in some way.

This might be a planetary ambition: a PC on every desk and in every home (Bill Gates); accelerate the world's transition to sustainable transportation (Elon Musk). But it's usually something more local. I have met a financial controller Pioneer who wants to change the way their firm does its month-end close; and a high school principal Pioneer who wants to redesign the curriculum in their school system to build more resilience into their students.

On average around the world, as you can see in Figure 4.1, there are more than two times the percentage of executive Pioneers as front-line Pioneers. The most extreme case is the United States, where there's a five times difference (30% of executives are Pioneers; only 6% of front line). In Western European countries and in Australia, it's on average a three times difference.

You may see this playing out in your own organization. A small group of leaders, with high degrees of influence, are motivated to change the norms and break the rules, in pursuit

	United States	Nigeria	Indonesia	Australia	India	China	Norway	Saudi Arabia	Brazil	Canada	Denmark	Japan
Share of Pioneers among Executives	30%	28%	24%	24%	23%	20%	20%	17%	15%	11%	7%	7%
Share of Pioneers among Corporate Frontline Workers	6%	21%	14%	9%	18%	8%	7%	11%	12%	7%	6%	6%

Figure 4.1 Mix of Pioneers among executives compared to frontline workers in 12 countries.

of challenging and ambitious goals. They manage and communicate with a much larger group of workers, the ones who touch customers every day, of whom only a small fraction are motivated by changing the world. The potential for misalignment, even conflict, is real.

I have spoken to hundreds of top leadership teams on these topics, and I ask them to take the quiz identifying the archetype they most closely resemble. It is common to see between 25% and even up to 40% of the group identify as Pioneers.

The Pioneer profile is well suited to certain types of corporate leadership roles, particularly in cultures that put a high value on leaders who challenge the status quo. There are also cultures where the typical Pioneer style is not effective in leadership. In Japan, for example, the well-established belief in compromise as a critical leadership skill is reflected in a very small mix of Pioneers in the executive ranks and a similar mix among workers overall: there is practically no gap at all.

The second striking difference is the mix of Operators: there are far more on the front line than in the executive ranks. Operators, remember, are the largest of the six archetype cohorts, in all countries. They want to do their job well but are not natural risk-takers. In fact, they often prefer to keep a low profile at work, enjoy the friendship of colleagues, and then get off work to focus on the things they prioritize more highly.

This is not to say Operator archetypes cannot be leaders. Marcia, a 60-year-old lawyer at a multinational firm in Brazil, said, "I never aimed for status or prestige in my work; this does not motivate me. God is what matters most to me and gives me purpose; after God is my family and kids and then maybe work."

I know a several-time CEO in the consumer goods industry who has never moved away from a 50-square-mile area in his home country because it kept him close to his parents, his spouse's family, his children's school, and, it turned out, their early career years. He turned down multiple roles to pursue his real ambition in life, to invest in his family and the community he was born into.

Operators value safety and security in their jobs – attributes that leadership roles cannot always promise. This is one reason they are more prone to stress at work, as discussed in Chapter 5.

Executives are much more satisfied with their jobs, and with their lives overall, compared to frontline workers. They are also more stressed at work (remember Datini). And they are much more comfortable taking risks to try to improve their lives, even if the risk could leave them worse off.

More satisfied, more risk-tolerant, and more stressed: what is up with executives? The first thought is that they are usually getting paid more, which may help mitigate some of the stress and the risk-taking. The second is that an extraordinarily high proportion (41%) of the most highly stressed executives are *also* highly satisfied with their job. Among frontline workers, that number is just 21%. Executives are two times more likely to be highly stressed *and* highly satisfied compared to the workers they manage.

The most valuable job attributes that executives look for are not so different from what others want. For men, they are good compensation, flexibility, job security, and interesting work. For women executives, their top four includes good relationships, which is more important than interesting work, and a lot more important to them than it is to men.

Women Leaders

There are libraries of excellent work on the pitiful under-representation of women in top leadership positions, despite their increased presence in the workforce and their proven capabilities as leaders. Leadership has historically been associated with "masculine" traits such as assertiveness, decisiveness, and competitiveness, while "feminine" traits like empathy and collaboration have been undervalued in traditional business settings.

Organizational structures and practices perpetuate gender inequality in leadership. Male-dominated networks can limit access to mentorship, sponsorship, and career advancement opportunities for women. As discussed in Chapter 6, work cultures that prioritize long hours and face time can disadvantage women.

Our research has important insight to contribute to this discussion. We know that around the world, the overall archetype mix of women at work is almost exactly the same as it is for men. On average, motivations at work are gender blind. In the executive ranks, however, there are many more female Givers than male (27% versus 20%). This would be the conventional prediction, and it is true: a higher proportion of women than of men are succeeding in leadership roles with the more supportive, empathetic, team-oriented leadership style we associate with Givers (although let us not ignore the fact that one male executive in five is also a Giver).

But this is *by no means the only model* for female leaders. The motivations of female executives result in a slightly higher mix of Pioneers, the same mix of Explorers, and a slightly lower mix of Strivers as their male counterparts. Proportionately, there are as many women leaders as men drawing on the "change the world" energy of the Pioneer, the "enthusiastic freedom seeking" energy of the Explorer, and the "keep driving forward" motivating energy of the Striver.

Women leaders already know that they are not all alike when it comes to motivations and styles. If we could run the archetype and motivation research on Mary Barra (CEO, General Motors), Lisa Su (CEO, AMD), Roz Brewer (former CEO of Walgreens Boots Alliance), Jane Fraser (CEO, Citigroup), Ana Botin (executive chair, Santander Group), Safra Catz (CEO, Oracle), Vicki Hollub (CEO, Occidental Petroleum), Joey Watt (CEO, Yum China), Michelle Buck (CEO, Hershey), Debra Crew (CEO, Diageo), Margherita Della Valle (CEO, Vodafone), Greta Gerwig (actress, screenwriter, film director), Kathryn Bigelow (filmmaker), Ursula von der Leyen (president, European Commission), Christine Lagarde (president, European Central Bank), Taylor Swift (singer-songwriter), MacKenzie Scott (philanthropist, novelist), Janet Yellen (Secretary of the Treasury, United States), Dong Mingzhu (president, Gree Electric), Makiko Ono (CEO, Suntory), Choi Soo-yeon (CEO, Naver) . . . or any of the countless thousands of exceptional women leaders, does anyone really believe that we would find them all to be motivated in the same way, by all the same things, in the same exact proportions?

Archetype thinking can release us from oversimplified, restrictive assumptions and biases.

Mind the Gaps

Archetype profiles differ between executives and other workers. So what? Should one group change its motivation to look more like the other? Or suppress its true motivations to appear more like the other? Of course not.

Leaders from the old norms did generally assume that those they led would behave as they did. (Remember "Would you like to get ahead in this world? Then learn how to please your boss" from Chapter 1?) They projected a Striver mindset onto their workers and, with it, the assumption that everyone was trying to get ahead, to move up through the hierarchy just like they had.

Today's new norms leaders are aware of the biases embedded in their leadership teams as a function of archetype mix. A 12-person leadership team with six Pioneers, three Explorers, two Strivers, and a single Giver risks total disconnection from the voice of the Operators and Artisans on their teams (around 40% of the typical workforce). Even the Giver can be part of the problem: it is often part of their role to make sure this top team is high functioning. They will be the one organizing "Top Team Alignment" workshops, even though the top team does not represent the workers it must inspire and manage to get anything done.

A winning leadership team invests to understand in detail the archetype composition of the workers they lead. This awareness will allow them to navigate three predictable tensions.

Tension 1: Hours and Workload

The first tension is about hours and workload. As you will see in Chapter 5, these are the two most energy-draining sources of stress at work. Pioneers in the executive ranks can be quite comfortable with long hours and regard the stress that accompanies them as a necessary part of their journey to change the world. Striver leaders will endure long hours and heavy workloads so long as they are in service of career advancement and help them to deliver results for which they anticipate later rewards. For others, not so much. The middle of dinnertime WhatsApp or Wechat starting "Where are the ...?"; the evening vigils at the keyboard; the 9:50 p.m. emails not explicitly asking for but in reality asking for immediate attention – these are among the stressors that lead other archetypes down the tunnel to dissatisfaction.

Tension 2: Language and Communication

The second tension is about language and communications. The next time a leader rises to talk at the town hall or the daily standup or the annual holiday party, an appreciation for their own biases and the mix of the audience will help them design messages to engage everyone. For example, what sounds fine to a Pioneer, that "Here at Acme Co., we must be in permanent transformation in order to stay competitive," is guaranteed to scare some archetypes and turn others off.

Disruptions of known routines are energy-sapping for all but the most risk-comfortable and change-tolerant. Constant change requires significant energy and leaves little time for replenishment. A more effective message for Operators, Givers, and Artisans might be "70% of your job is the same" not "30% of your job is different." Strivers want to hear that future plans will create new opportunities for contribution, advancement, and recognition. Explorers will respond to the idea that the future at Acme Co. needs flexible workers willing to build new skills and take on new assignments to meet changing customer needs.

Furthermore, if the message of permanent transformation is wrapped up in the idea that at Acme Co. the most important goal is for everyone to find their personal meaning and purpose in their work, most Operators tune out straightaway, and only a segment of the other archetypes are motivated by that ambition.

Tension 3: Differing Attitudes to Risk

The third tension involves attitudes to risk. Although different in so many ways, the Operator and the Striver are united in their broad aversion to taking risks at work. Taking risks does not sit comfortably with the Operator's desire to get their work done so that they can leave and focus on the things that really motivate their lives. Strivers do not welcome risk because it might introduce unknowns into their carefully planned-out future. Artisans become more risk averse as their career progresses, once they feel they have established credibility in their areas of expertise.

On the other hand, as we have seen, Pioneers are fine with risk, and many of them seek it out. Likewise, Explorers are comfortable taking risks with work, so long as they see the potential payoff in the chance for more variety or more autonomy.

We can find Givers on both sides of the risk-tolerant/risk-intolerant divide, but one thing we do know is that Givers do not lean toward risk-taking when it's only about advancing their own careers. Their source of energy is helping others to flourish; in the right situation, they might take a risk to do more of that.

■ ■ ■

Leaders are in a constant battle for energy in their organizations. Entropy hovers around every initiative they launch. All systems degenerate toward disorder unless more energy is introduced. They are permanently confronting the next imperative: digital; tariffs and sanctions; de-risking China; climate change; war in Ukraine; inflation; Environmental, Social, and Governance (ESG); supply chain disruption; AI. They are always choosing where and how to direct the energy of the organization. Sloan channeled GM's energy to the car divisions where designers, manufacturers, and marketers converged: he used the systems, processes, routines, and committees to remove as much friction as possible between them and the parts of the organization that did not face customers directly. Datini's entrepreneurial resilience, plus his hands-on leadership, even as he pivoted time and time again, were the sources of his businesses' energy.

Leaders are often hardworking, risk-seeking (or at least, risk-tolerant), well paid, highly stressed, yet highly satisfied. No wonder they are frustrated when coworkers appear risk-averse, low energy, and locked into the status quo. If they understand the rich diversity of worker motivations, they can avoid the false assumptions that lead to tensions and use their understanding to shape good jobs and high-performing teams.

Chapter 5

Energy, Stress, and Wellness

In the book's introduction, I described how the bonds between firm and worker are loosening, and the edges of the firm becoming more translucent. There is one trend, however, that is moving to tighten those bonds. At the center of that trend is worker health.

I'm unsure whether Francesco Datini and Alfred P. Sloan spent any time ruminating on the stress of their coworkers (although I am willing to bet this was the last thing on the mind of Frederick Taylor). Here, we should draw a distinction between what we now loosely refer to as "health" (involving physical and mental and sometimes spiritual well-being) and what has for a long time been called "safety" at work. I cannot know, but do assume Sloan cared greatly about the safety of his crews in the manufacturing and assembly plants of General Motors. "Healthy" has become a defining attribute of a good job only quite recently, and this is related to the broadly based consumer movement toward improved health for all across many dimensions, including diet, exercise, rest, friendships, and mindfulness. This trend was further boosted in many countries by the pandemic. In one study in the United States,[1] as an example, almost half of all consumers agreed or strongly agreed that "I care much more about my physical and mental health now than I did before the COVID-19 pandemic started."

While there are still plenty of firms that do not see much need to play a role in their workers' health and some who find the idea an unacceptable invasion of privacy or a breach of the worker/firm contract, for the firms who are embracing a wellness agenda, there is solid logic to support their position.

Work stress can have serious negative impacts and lead to burnout, disengagement, employee turnover, and mental health problems. Firms want us to bring our healthiest selves to work. They will no doubt keep a sharp lookout for concrete results, in productivity data especially, but wellness at work is now a topic for conversation and investment – from ergonomic chairs to standing desks to healthier food in the cafeteria to gym membership reimbursement programs all the way to sleeping pods, meditation rooms, and on-site performance coaches (at least in the rarified working conditions that Carolyn Chen observed in Silicon Valley).[2] Support for counseling and other mental health treatment has also become more common.

Stress at work is on the rise. Gallup has been measuring it since 2009. In 2023, 41% of workers said they had experienced it (down slightly from a record high 44% in 2022). The metric Gallup is most known for, employee engagement, is defined as the "involvement and enthusiasm of employees in their work and workplace." This equaled its record high in 2023, the still depressingly low 23%.[3]

So, almost twice as many workers are stressed as are "involved and enthusiastic."

We set out to understand what the important stressors at work are. As always, the ambition was to de-average workers, because we know from experience that different people are stressed by different things. We also know stress that originates outside work can have an impact on performance and satisfaction at work.

At the same time, we wanted to understand the sources of energy for different types of worker. Energy is one of the opposites of stress. While it would be convenient to assume firms obeyed the first law of thermodynamics – energy can neither be created nor destroyed inside an isolated system – we cannot, because the humans who show up at work every day are the same humans who go home to be family members and friends, who go shopping as consumers, and who engage in their communities as citizens. The firm is not an isolated system. Firms can capture the energy created by individuals outside work. They do not pay for it, but they reap the benefit, with the conscious or unconscious cooperation of the individuals themselves.

If they can understand the sources of energy and stress at work, firms can construct programs and policies to help their people find a healthy balance *and* deliver better business results. Those sources are not the same for everyone, and based on Gallup's numbers, the assumption that they are is leaving 77% of workers either not engaged or actively disengaged.

What Is Stressing People Out at Work?

Stress is an equal opportunity illness – 19% of workers in our research report being *highly stressed*. This is the case for men and women, for younger workers and older workers. As you saw in Chapter 4, for executives, the highly stressed mix is almost twice the global average, at 34%.

These are the four most commonly cited causes of stress:

- Overall workload
- Long hours

Energy, Stress, and Wellness

- Worries about job security
- Being compensated fairly in comparison to others

These four stressors vary little across genders and markets, although in Japan, conflict with peers or bosses is the second highest ranked source of stress, where in other countries it is far down the list. The behavior preference in Japanese business is often to avoid conflict even when angry. People might downplay their own preferences, and perhaps use silence or the language of humility rather than express frustration out loud.

Executives share the same stressors. Overall workload, job security, and long hours are their clear top three.

We tested many potential causes, including boredom, irregular hours, being unsure how to do your job, and not being aligned with your company's mission. None was nearly as important as the top four.

For many, work is a grind. Those John Maynard Keynes predictions[4] have not materialized. The "quiet quitting" and "lying flat" and "lazy girl job" memes are a reaction to heavy workload combined with uncertain economic prospects and job insecurity. For many, the always-on communication demands from email, WhatsApp, WeChat, instant messaging/chat apps like Slack or Teams, document collaboration tools like Google workspace, internal blogs, file-sharing platforms like Dropbox or Microsoft OneDrive, project management apps like Asana or Trello, knowledge center platforms like SharePoint or Confluence . . . for many, these are the corporate equivalents of toxic social media.

The archetype lens helps us understand the diverse experience of stress. More Operators (almost one in four of them) are highly stressed than any other archetype, while Givers and Explorers have the lowest mix of high-stress workers.

All archetypes consider workload and long hours the top two drivers of stress. Operators have a high spike on conflict with peers or bosses at work. You will remember that Operators like to have friends at work, generally prefer to keep a low profile, and take few risks – this stress data is further evidence for the distinctive features of the Operator.

Meanwhile, Pioneers and Explorers report that overall workload and long hours contribute to their stress at much higher levels than for the other archetypes. Strivers show a stress spike on being fairly compensated relative to others – confirmation of their job attribute ranking examined in Chapter 2, where we saw Strivers to be the archetype that most highly prioritizes good compensation.

Life Stressors

We explored sources of stress in life, too, knowing the interplay between work and life that I mentioned in the introduction to this chapter. The answers here were clear. Two sources overshadow all others we tested:

- Worries about money
- Worries about health and aging

The answers were the same for men and women, for workers of different age groups (older workers unsurprisingly ranked health concerns a bit ahead of money concerns), for different countries, and for different archetypes (Strivers and Pioneers were more concerned about career failure than the others). Compared to these, trends in geopolitics, the impact of AI, crime and violence, the effects of climate change, the daily demands of work – all these and others were of much lower importance as stressors in life.

Highly Stressed, Yet Highly Satisfied

In general, feelings of satisfaction and loyalty to your employer decline as stress at work increases. As always, we should take notice of the general and then de-average. There is a cohort who are highly stressed at work *yet* highly satisfied *and* loyal. I described highly satisfied stress-prone, or even stress-seeking, leaders in Chapter 4, but it's broader than that: 22% of all workers describe themselves as "high stress high satisfaction." It's slightly higher for men than women, and it's higher for older workers than younger ones.

The archetypes are different here: 35% of the highly stressed Pioneers are also highly satisfied. The Pioneer's typical ambition, to change the world in some way, turns out to be really hard – but very satisfying if you think you are on your way to doing it.

Among Strivers, the high stress/high satisfaction mix is only 20%. Strivers plan ahead and are less likely to be risk-takers. They would rather keep moving up the organization in predictable steps. They want to work hard and achieve promotions and recognition and the compensation raises that come with them. When their stressors are triggered (overall workload, long hours, and compensation worries), this strikes at the core of why Strivers go to work, and they are much less likely to be satisfied.

When Work Fuels Energy

On the flip side of high-stress workers are the low- and no-stress workers and those who find energy at work. Feeling confident in your ability to do your job is the number-one most important source of energy, followed by job security, seeing results from the work you do, and doing work that interests you. These four stand far ahead of all the other sources we tested.

The results are broadly consistent across genders, countries, job levels, and archetypes, with a few differences to note. Strivers and Operators value job security most highly as an energy source. Artisans rank having friends at work much lower than the other archetypes. Pioneers are more energized by having opportunities to learn and grow. Both Pioneers and Givers derive more energy than the others from the positive impact of their firm's mission and vision (although on average, this is the least important source of energy of all the ones we tested – more on this later). These results are well aligned with everything we have learned about the six archetypes.

Helping Workers Manage Their Stress

What can firms do to help their workers manage stress and create energy at work? We tested 11 different types of programs for their impact on wellness. Our workers reported that they were typically offered between 3 and 4 of the 11.

The number of programs and policies offered made essentially no difference to the level of stress each worker was experiencing. In other words, stress at work for someone offered no wellness support programs is the same as for someone offered six or more different options. *However*, the number of programs offered made a very big difference to satisfaction and to loyalty. The more wellness programs on offer, the more satisfied and more loyal the worker feels, even if the programs are not doing much to actually help with the stress. This is true for the workforce overall *and* for the high-stress workers described earlier.

In terms of which specific programs have the most impact, as you would expect, there are different preferences at the individual level. For some, it is the subsidy of a yoga course at the local gym; for others, the chance to spend a few hours a week on a passion project; for yet others, the underwriting of team social events. Overall, the strong consensus was that offering flexible hours when needed and having a worker-friendly leave of absence or time-off program were by far the two most valuable offers.

There is a measurable value to flexibility. People will trade off less compensation for more of it. It is no surprise people leaders are trying to define what flexibility means in their organizations while also preventing flexibility from tipping over into unproductive chaos.

Remote work policies are a case in point. The millions of discussion hours expended on this topic before, during, and since the pandemic have yet to produce a consensus view, and probably never will. Individuals want what they want: in our research, about one quarter say they never want to go back to an office again, one quarter say they never want to work from home again, and the remaining half are more or less equally split between working remotely one, two, three, or four days. There are many domestic factors at play: commute time, stability of Internet reception at home, size of the home, and number of other people living in it.

Research studies have been called into service on all sides of the debate: Remote work is more productive; no, it's less productive. Hybrid work leads to higher employee satisfaction; no, it leads to lower satisfaction. Remote work leads to negative impacts on innovation, collaboration, and culture; no, if we adjust metrics, goal setting, and ways of working for a remote/ hybrid world, there is no negative impact.

Industry sector details matter here, to define what is and what is not possible. The consistent themes from more recent studies are that employees value flexibility; that they believe they are as or more productive when working remotely; that in hybrid arrangements the best people to make decisions about which days to collocate are team members and team leaders (not the CEO); and that the trend is for firms to be pushing more people back into the office for more days a week.

Our first waves of research were mid-COVID-19, in 2021 and 2022. The most recent wave was in early 2024. We can compare worker perspectives on remote work across those two periods, which has as its backdrop the effective end of the pandemic and a nonstop litany of announcements about remote work policies.

The headlines are simple: on average globally during COVID-19, about 25% of workers said they wanted to work remotely all the time. In 2024, it's still the same proportion. More younger workers tend to prefer fully remote, but otherwise there are negligible differences between women and men, high income and low income, highly educated and less educated.

There are, however, major differences from country to country. In the United States, for example, 56% of workers prefer four or five days a week working remotely. In China, the equivalent number is 26%. Being a people leader in a multinational firm gets harder and harder.

To restate the main point of this book – when we de-average employees, we can design work and jobs around business objectives *and* what motivates the worker. This will include where and when work gets done.

Should Firms Take a Stand on Political and Social Topics?

Brian Armstrong, the CEO of Coinbase, a cryptocurrency exchange platform, made the news in September 2020 when he sent a memo to the employees outlining a new policy: Coinbase would strive to be an apolitical company. It would not engage in activism or take a stance on political or social issues unrelated to its business ambition, to build the infrastructure for a more open financial system.[5]

The memo landed at a time when many firms were actively taking positions on social issues, from racial justice to climate change. Armstrong believed activism could be divisive and detrimental to his company's focus.

He argued that taking a stance on every social issue would distract Coinbase from its primary goal, and potentially alienate customers who held different views. In the memo, he wrote that while Coinbase would still welcome discussions and diverse viewpoints internally, it would not engage in activism or political debates publicly. He emphasized the importance of staying focused on their goals and not getting sidetracked by external pressures.

Some applauded Armstrong for prioritizing the company's mission and maintaining a neutral stance. Others accused him of ignoring important social issues and shirking corporate responsibility.[6]

There are firms lined up on either side of this debate. In April 2021, Basecamp, a small project management software company, announced a policy banning political discussions at work.[7] Like Armstrong, the company's founders said that they wanted Basecamp to focus solely on work-related matters and avoid distractions. There was some reporting at the time that around one-third of Basecamp's employees took a buyout and left the firm in protest.

On the other flank there are celebrated firms such as Patagonia, the outdoor clothing and gear company whose founder we met earlier, which has always taken strong, visible positions on climate change, public lands protection, and sustainable business practices. Or Ben & Jerry's, the ice-cream brand owned by Unilever, which advocates for racial justice, LGBTQ+ rights, climate change, and campaign finance reform.

This is a live debate. It's common to hear from leaders on these topics, which is precisely why we wanted to ask workers at all levels and in all job types if their firms have an obligation to take a stance on these issues. The results were startling. American workers were *least likely* to agree. Just 37% said Yes to the question (and that was down from 44% in 2021). Perhaps there is fatigue in the United States with the polarization of opinions on a wide range of social issues, and workers want work to be a safe space. That is one way to interpret the Coinbase approach: shut down the discussion and you might suppress the potential conflict too. Or perhaps the media bullhorn amplifies each incident where management and workers are at odds on a social topic, concealing the fact that two-thirds of American workers do not need their firm to voice an opinion.

In other mature democracies like France and Japan, 71% responded yes to whether firms have an obligation to take a stance on issues. But the largest difference by far was between the United States and China, where fully 83% of workers believe their firm should take a stance.

A first instinctive reaction might be to assume the influence of the Chinese Communist Party (CCP). The CCP does have thoroughly documented corporate social responsibility goals, which describe socially responsible activities in support of the

Party's agenda, such as poverty alleviation, environmental protection, and the promotion of Chinese culture. And it is true, the CCP exerts significant influence on private companies as well as on state-owned enterprises.

This might be a serious underestimation of Chinese workers. They are social media fluent and willing to bring pressure as activists on a broad range of topics. There have been high-visibility, widespread worker protests against gender discrimination in the Chinese tech industry, for example, calling out individual firms for not doing enough to protect female employees. In 2018, ride-hailing leader Didi Chuxing – after the tragic murder of two female passengers by drivers using the platform – also faced high-decibel employee complaints.[8] The firm changed its safety measures: improving background checks on drivers, changing emergency response mechanisms, and increasing passenger education about safety features.

Some employees found this insufficient. They organized more protests and launched online campaigns to send unambiguous messages to management. They demanded greater transparency, improved communication channels between employees and leadership, and a stronger commitment to passenger safety, all of which they eventually got.

Optimism

Stress, energy and wellness. It's a lot. It's a lot for us to work on individually. It's a lot for a firm to tackle on behalf of all its workers. Pouring over our data about stress, stressing about it, I realized that I had overlooked an important question from the research. In the face of all their challenges at work – the grind, work overload, long hours, inflexible time-off policies, conflicts with bosses and peers, not feeling confident about doing the job well – three-quarters of the 48,000 workers we talked to said they were nevertheless optimistic their life would be better in the next 5–10 years. In some countries, it was much higher than that: India 87%, Brazil and Saudi Arabia 89%, China and UAE 91%, Nigeria 93%, and Indonesia 94%. (You will not miss the shared characteristics in that group of seven economies: fast growing and mostly younger workforces.)

A powerful source of energy at work may simply be optimism. Optimists put the work in. Optimistic Strivers strive, Explorers explore, Givers give, and so on. Pessimists, on the other hand, often disengage from the work. Some simple, "back-of-the-envelope" calculations demonstrate why this is important. According to Gallup, in 2023, 15% of global workers are "actively disengaged."[9] I make the assumption that most of those are pessimists. If I then compare the 23% of workers who tell Gallup they are "actively engaged" with the 75% of workers who tell us they are optimistic, we reveal just over 50% who are optimistic but "not engaged."

That is the opportunity, and the obligation we share: to unlock the optimism and energy of half the world's workers.

Energy, Stress, and Wellness

Chapter 6

Older and Younger, Women and Men

In the book's introduction, I made two assertions in support of the fundamental claim that de-averaging workers will lead to more good jobs for more people and, therefore, better firm results through higher satisfaction and better productivity. The first point was that workers are not all the same at work; in fact, they want different things, apply different weightings to elements of a job, and have their own models to make decisions about what's important to them at work. The second was that it is an unsupported assumption that every worker is trying to move up the hierarchy of their organization in the same way.

These assertions rely on the self-reported attitude and preference data our research has gathered. Those attitudes and preferences are invisible until you ask about them. It turns out that two of the more visible differences between workers – age and gender – already provide significant and actionable insight on how to make more good jobs.

Older Workers

In Nancy Mayers's 2015 film *The Intern*, 70-year-old Ben Whittaker (played by Robert De Niro) applies for an internship at online fashion insurgent *About the Fit*, whose CEO Jules Ostin (Anne Hathaway) has agreed the firm should participate in a program encouraging seniors back into the workforce.

Ben submits a video application: "I love the idea of having a place I can go every day," he says to camera, "I want the connection, the excitement. I want to be challenged, and I guess I might even want to be needed. The tech stuff might take a bit to figure out, but I'll get there."

Ben's video earns him an invitation into the office for an in-person interview with enthusiastic young hiring manager, Justin (Natt Wolf).

"Now," says Justin, "I'm going to ask you one of our more telling questions. This is one to really think about . . . and take your time . . . where do you see yourself in 10 years?."

Ben pauses, "When I'm . . . 80?"

Things work out well for Ben. He gets the internship. He loses, then wins back, Jules's trust in the office and in what turns out to be her complicated domestic life. He ends up giving her critical advice about whether to hire an outside CEO (we might more normally have expected her to consult the lead investors or her board, but hey, it's a movie). By the end of the film they are practicing tai chi together. Oh, and widower Ben finds a new relationship at work too.

I'm a big fan of the film. And therefore I am sorry to report that this is not the typical experience of 70 year olds at work. For people like Ben, what exactly is "the fit"?

The Workforce Is Aging

This is not a matter of idle curiosity. Populations are aging; work lives are lengthening. Fewer young people are entering the workforce, due to lower fertility rates and more time spent in education. A long-term trend toward earlier retirement is going into reverse.

The late-eighteenth/early nineteenth-century English economist, Thomas Malthus, confidently predicted that as people
became wealthier, they would have more children. This has
turned out to be not simply wrong but the inverse of the truth.
In rich and middle-income countries across the world, fertility rates are below – often far below and with no prospect of
reversing – the population replacement rate of 2.1 children
per woman.[1]

This demographic and workforce reality has been better understood and more publicly discussed over the last few years.
While there is still plenty of rightful fascination with Gen Z and
how they are behaving at work, more and more attention is
being paid to older workers.

The United Kingdom increased its retirement age from 60
(for women) and 65 (for men), first by equalizing genders and
then pushing both to 66, with a plan to raise still further from
2026.[2] France endured political disturbance when President
Macron pushed through an increase from 62 to 64.[3] Prior to
a recent increase, the Japanese government struggled for decades to raise the official retirement age, leaving firms to address
the topic themselves by releasing workers at 60 and rehiring
them on new contracts, often at reduced pay rates.[4] Singapore,
like the United Kingdom, is taking a progressive approach: in
2022 it raised the minimum retirement age to 63 with a plan to
keep raising it to 65 by 2030.[5]

We project that in the Group of Seven countries (Canada,
France, Germany, Italy, Japan, the United Kingdom, and the
United States), workers aged 55 and older will exceed 25% of
the workforce by 2031, nearly 10 percentage points higher than
in 2011. Put another way, when your "two pizza" team is working late, two of the eight of them will be over 55. Japan is the

Older and Younger, Women and Men

current extreme. By 2031, Japanese workers 55 and older will approach 40% of the workforce. European countries led by Italy are catching up to Japan with considerable speed, prompting immigration policy shifts unthinkable a generation ago.

During COVID-19, there was a disturbance in the workforce in a number of countries, which earned the title of the Great Resignation. In hindsight, it was more of a Great Sabbatical, a blip in the long-term trend data, with a higher percentage of retirees now reentering the workforce than in February 2019. According to Gallup, 41% of American workers now expect to work beyond age 65. Thirty years ago, it was 12%.[6]

This is not an issue only for developed markets. Brazil's proportion of workers over 55 is creeping up to the mid-teens. China, where retirement age is very low compared to mature economies (50 years for blue collar females, 55 for white collar females, 60 years for males) inter-generational conflict is inevitable as population decline puts unsustainable pressure on those in work. In many other parts of Asia, it is the rate at which aging is accelerating that causes most concern. The progression from 7% of the population over 65 years to 14% – usually considered the threshold for an aged society – is happening in 15–20 years in multiple Asian countries. That same journey took more than a century in most western European countries and more than 70 years in the United States.

Added up globally, approximately 150 million jobs will shift to workers 55 and older by the end of this decade. Organizations will have no choice: they are going to be managing older talent.

Despite the shift, it's been relatively rare to see organizations put programs in place to integrate older workers into their talent system. In a global employer survey from 2020, the

American Association of Retired Persons (AARP) found fewer than 4% of firms were already committed to such programs, with a further 27% saying they were "very likely" to explore them in the future.[7]

More recently, there are signs of change: in France a group of high-profile companies (L'Oréal, Galeries Lafayette, Pernod Ricard, Air France, Sodexo, and AXA, to name just a few of the 40+ companies already enrolled) have signed up to the charter of Club Landoy, a collective created in 2019 that acts to make the demographic transition a catalyst for social innovation.[8] The signatory firms commit to measure their recruiting, training, employment, and mobility for older workers.

The good news is that, with the right tools and mindset, aging workforces can help employers get ahead of their talent gaps and create high-quality jobs that turn older workers' skills into sources of competitive advantage. There's persuasive Organization for Economic Cooperation and Development (OECD) research from 2020[9] concluding that age-diverse firms are lower in turnover and higher in productivity than benchmarks.

Of course, there are challenges. Not all jobs are equal when it comes to age diversity: it's quite easy to picture an academic or a store greeter working deep into their seventies, but this may be harder to imagine for a roof repairer or delivery van driver. Not all career changes can be made quickly or easily: after a 30-year career as an accountant, few are going to re-skill as research scientists. Not all older workers are the same: their motivations are their own, so we must not assume older workers fit a singular profile.

The shift will demand new skills and new systems. Firms have been living in a world of talent scarcity for a while and

Older and Younger, Women and Men

have spent decades learning to do more with fewer people. The encouragement of self-managing teams, the slimming down of middle management, the increased use of networks and ecosystem partners, and, above all, the continuous investment in productivity gains through technology – all of these are standard parts of the modern firm's playbook.

But with older workers, there is inevitably another dimension to the response. We have parents whose attitudes and motivations at work may have influenced our own. We all age and take note of the range of impacts that aging has on motivation and performance in ourselves and colleagues.

On the one hand, some brands want us to believe that 60 is the new 40. We are bombarded with stories about wealthy fanatics investing in life-extending protocols of diet and supplements, keen to treat death as a curable illness. Attractive 60 year olds beam out from the ads encouraging us to carefully protect heirloom assets for our children. The medical establishment reminds us to take up kitesurfing or learn piano or do more crossword puzzles – all in the interests of staving off mental deterioration as we age.

On the other hand, we live in an era of widespread age discrimination. Study after study around the world reports that a typical range of 30–35% of workers have personally experienced some form of age discrimination at work, and a much larger number (often 60% or higher) report seeing age discrimination at their firm.[10] This is despite anti-discrimination legislation being on the books in many countries.

While governments can certainly help, through immigration policies that help fill vacant jobs and retirement laws that encourage longer work spans, it will mostly fall to firms to evolve long-entrenched practices that have disadvantaged older workers. Our research into worker archetypes can help.

What Older Workers Want

The unsurprising insight that our research reveals is that what older people want at work is not always the same as workers of other age groups. The surprising insight is that older workers are not all different in the same way.

Before I get to some data, consider what exactly defines an older worker. We could not find a good answer to that. Some studies use age itself, which does not properly take type of work into account. Others use number of years away from standard retirement age and mostly settle on 10 years away as defining "older."

There are aspects to any definition that are situational. Tom Brady was an older worker as a 45-year-old quarterback in the NFL. Colonel Harland Sanders founded Kentucky Fried Chicken at the age of 65. Perceptions about when we cross over into "older" can be highly personal.

We have not tried to establish a precise definition. We have simply let the global data lead us to notice at what ages motivations and job attribute priorities start to change – or at least, start to change for many people. I want to stress that there are workers we have talked to who stay exactly who they are at work over their entire careers. Their archetype does not change. Once again, firms need to de-average their view. We have uncovered actionable insights about what older workers want in general, but in reality older workers are diverse in their archetypes, just like middle-aged and younger ones.

Starting around 55 years, we see three interrelated changes in the way workers prioritize job attributes.

The importance of good compensation starts to decline (prior to this, as we have seen, good compensation has been the most important element of a job in most markets, across genders and archetypes). The importance of interesting work and of autonomy starts to grow.

By the time workers reach 60, these trends are still accelerating. Interesting work has become the number-one attribute, and autonomy has spiked up into the top fourth or fifth position, depending on the country.

For context, among 25 year olds, interesting work is a top attribute for 16% of workers. At 75, the oldest workers in our research, that has jumped to 31%.

The increasing desire for autonomy at work is often expressed in efforts to control hours. Far more older workers now, compared to a generation ago, say they plan to reduce their working hours in preparation for retirement.

Managing the transition to fewer hours might come through working part-time, self-employment, or doing freelance work. Our research shows a significant increase in these forms of employment among the 55-and-over age group, compared to people in midcareer.

While we spotlight interesting work and autonomy, let us not ignore workers who do not have the luxury to reprioritize as they age. For example, Godwin, a manufacturer of house paint in Nigeria, said, "People in Nigeria normally retire at age 65. I'm 63, but I'm nowhere close to retirement because I have nothing to retire on."

Here is Lalu, 62, owner and operator of a small restaurant in India, who said, "COVID-19 disrupted my life in a way I never expected it to. I lost my job and had to shift back to my hometown and start a small eating joint with the help of my wife. Rising fuel and food prices barely allow me to manage my expenses."

There are also variations to these averages when we dig down to the country level. While interesting work becomes the number-one most important job attribute for workers 60 and over in many countries (France, Italy, Germany, United Kingdom, Australia, and Japan, for example), it's not the case everywhere. In China, flexibility is first. In India, it's job security. Only in the United States does good compensation remain the number-one job attribute even for older workers.

Archetypes evolve with age too. In aggregate the change is dramatic (I repeat, this does not mean everyone's archetype will change as they grow older). Strivers and Pioneers when young become Givers and Artisans with age. By age 68, more than 50% of our global workers are Givers or Artisans, compared to just 30% at age 28.

You will recall that Artisans are primarily motivated by mastering their craft. They want to do work that interests them, and they value the autonomy to get on with it. For Givers, work is about service. They feel rewarded by seeing their actions make a positive impact in the lives of others.

Some companies have adapted their talent programs to meet these different needs of older workers. Home Depot was early to see the opportunity. It partnered with AARP in the United States in 2004 to recruit and train workers 55 and older.[11] Just a few months after the program launched, 11,000 older workers had applied, and more than 1,000 positions were filled.

Mitsubishi Corporation in Japan created a Career Design Center exclusively for employees aged 60 and older, offering custom training, job matching, and individual consultation services for senior workers. Tokyo Gas has its Grand Career System, with similar objectives, for all employees over 50. The program provides career development support, training, and one-on-one mentoring. As a result, more than 90% of Tokyo Gas workers facing mandatory retirement were rehired by the company or its subsidiaries. These two examples are about

Older and Younger, Women and Men

designing roles suited for an older worker while still recognizing the intrinsic motivations of each individual.

The National Institutes of Health (NIH) in the United States actively recruits people looking for a second career, often ex-military and ex-academia. As of 2013, nearly half of the NIH workforce was over 50. The NIH has been recognized as one of the best places for older workers, thanks to their flexible work policies, opportunities to mentor younger colleagues, and health programs.[12]

Older workers attach surprisingly little importance to learning and growth. Just 3% of those aged 55 and over rate it as a top motivator. Some believe they are already fit for the work, with 29% of the 55-to-64 group saying they do not need new skills.

It's true that older workers do not get invited to training programs as much as younger colleagues, but in the United States at least, more than half are offered training every year.

Both workers and employers need to shift their thinking on retraining. The absence of a growth mindset in an older worker might make them a weak candidate for extended employment. But companies need to design training programs that appeal. Older workers are motivated to participate when training helps to accelerate their pursuit of interesting work.

There are success stories. Global technology firm Atos launched a program in 2021 to bridge the skill gaps of its 21,000 employees over the age of 50. Employees have to set goals and decide what courses, certifications, and training would benefit them – all provided free. Atos also called on its "tenured talent" as instructors in the programs.[13]

The Digital Skills Ready@50+ program developed with support from Google.org (Google's charitable foundation) and the AARP Foundation is a philanthropic response to one of the most obvious skill gaps. Google's grant to AARP for this program provides training to 25,000 people aged 50 and older who are low-income, particularly targeting women and people of color.[14]

Older workers tend to be more loyal to their employers; they also tend to be more satisfied at work and with life in general. The Givers like to mentor. The Artisans set high standards of performance for those around them. Creating space for older workers to bring their unique benefits to work can strengthen the culture for everyone.

BMW has considered the physical toll on assembly workers, and in 2007 made ergonomic adjustments on the line that helped older workers and improved overall productivity by 7%. In addition to those improvements, BMW's Senior Experts program sees retired workers return to the company part-time to share their expertise with younger colleagues.[15] This checks all the boxes for a certain archetype of older worker: autonomy, flexibility, and helping others succeed.

Marriott designed its Flex Options for hourly workers program, offering 325,000 older associates new roles that are less physically taxing.[16]

Allianz has gone all in. They understood that we have four and sometimes five generations at work today: Silent, Boomers, Gen X, Millennials, and Gen Z. A multigeneration team faces challenges that single age group teams do not. At the most basic level, how to communicate: Slack, WhatsApp, WeChat, email, phone, or live in-person? The norms for each generation are very different.

Armed with the simple facts about their workforce age profile, Allianz took a decisive view of age inclusion across the five generations and has built multiple programs, under the Allianz Engage banner, to help each generation thrive on its own terms, and to try to capture the benefits of cross-generation work.[17]

The uncomfortable truth is that age-related work discrimination is still widespread. Demographic reality will catch up with that attitude soon enough. And when it does, firms that invest in recruiting, reskilling, and respecting the strengths of older workers will not just solve a part of their talent gap problem, they'll create a workforce that's more productive, more balanced, more diverse, and more loyal than the one they have today.

Younger Workers

I have described changes to strategy and talent models as firms push deeper into this new era of business. Generational inertia is one reason these evolutions can take decades. It is natural to look at younger people for a sense of where things might be heading at work, which brings us to Gen Z.

I used the standard definition of Gen Z, those born between 1997 and 2012. The first thing that jumps out about this generation is that of those who are already working, only half have full-time jobs. Another quarter are working part-time, with the remaining quarter either self-employed or working on a contingent basis (perhaps gig work, or something contracted but nonpermanent and with lower security). We have noted before: contingent workers, especially at the low end of the income scale, are much less satisfied than workers doing the same work on a full-time basis.

Sure enough, low-income Gen Z workers are the least satisfied of any group we have heard from. This is not just compared to middle- and high-income Gen Zs, but to all other age and income groups.

The second observation is that COVID-19 had a significant impact on Gen Z at work. No surprise there. For the Gen Zs who joined a company after finishing education, the chances are they started work remotely and, depending on the type of work, might have had a couple of years barely meeting anyone from their firm in person. Flexible work schedules and remote work look normal to them, and they prefer hybrid working much more than older workers. In almost all developed and developing markets, two-thirds of the Gen Z workers report that COVID-19 changed their views on the need for balance between work and life, made it more likely they would consider a job move, and pushed them to consider other big changes in their lives (for example, moving cities). This is a much higher rate than for other age groups.

In global aggregate, the job attributes that Gen Z most value are highly comparable to those most important to Millennials (workers 55 years and over often have different priorities). One difference is learning and growth, which is two times more important to Gen Zs than to other age groups, and comes a close second to good compensation in their overall rankings.

There is also a difference in the archetype mix. There are lots more Gen Z Pioneers (13% versus 9% among Millennials), with both India and Nigeria having remarkably high Gen Z Pioneer mix, drafting off the underlying economic growth in those countries and giving workers confidence to want to change the world.

At the same time, Gen Z is stressed at work, more so than other age groups in almost all countries. They are less satisfied with their jobs and less satisfied with their lives. Despite the higher stress, lower satisfaction, and COVID-19 hangover, almost 80% of Gen Zs feel their lives will be better in 5–10 years' time. I touched on the superpower of human optimism in Chapter 5 – here it is again.

Older and Younger, Women and Men

If we enlarge the images of Gen Z, differences between countries begin to appear. America's Gen Z has been intensively studied. Among other things, they are said to see no clean divisions between work and the rest of their lives, to be keen on mass customization and hyper-personalization (they should value the changes to talent management that this book is arguing for), to be highly conscious of both environmental and social issues, and to be concerned for their physical and mental health. They care a lot about diversity in the firms they work at. COVID-19 certainly impacted American Gen Z's ranking of job priorities. In 2021, flexibility was most important; by the time we went back for another round of research in 2024, flexibility had become less important and, as in every other country of the world, good compensation was their number-one priority.

Chinese Gen Z look different. In fact, they are the opposite of other countries in many ways. They prefer more days working in the office. They feel less impacted by COVID-19 than older generations. They are less stressed than Millennials and Boomers, more satisfied with their jobs, and optimistic about the future. Yes, there are millions of Gen Z in China without jobs. Youth unemployment is relatively high. The Gen Zs we talked to in China do have jobs. The sons and daughters of Chinese born in the 1970s, they have grown up watching a sustained rise in prosperity, and they still see plenty of opportunity in a 3–5% growth economy. This is particularly true for people outside the Tier 1 "bubble" of Beijing/Shanghai/Guangzhou/Shenzhen, who may be less exposed to international media and less impacted by the wave of tech firm layoffs of the last few years. We should not confuse "lying flat" with a nationwide sense of hopelessness or pessimism in this generation. An increase in the Striver mix among China's Gen Z since 2021 might even suggest that slower than expected post-COVID-19 recovery is firing ambition in some.

Japan is also an outlier, right across the workforce, including Gen Z. Japanese workers have tended to be highly stressed, quite dissatisfied with their jobs, and not at all optimistic about the future. The three "lost decades" (into which all Japanese Gen Zs were born) of flat or declining real wages, barely perceptible economic growth, and low levels of government investment in talent development have taken a toll. There has been little for the average young worker to be excited about. But now, there is a sense of change among Gen Z and Millennial workers. More full-time jobs are being created. There is more willingness to move jobs for better opportunities, more courage to ask for more in the new roles, more pressure eroding the lifetime employment model, and more energy behind elevating women in senior roles. The aging, shrinking workforce may yet turn out to be the trigger for long-awaited improvements at work for younger Japanese.

From these examples, in the three largest economies, we see that a single Gen Z proposition will not travel successfully around the world. We need a more nuanced view of younger workers – just as we do of older workers – to create good jobs for them. For Gen Z, we must ask the question, how much are they influenced by their generation and how much by their archetype?

The answer based on this work is that the motivations of each archetype are more important. A Gen Z Operator has more in common with a Millennial Operator than with a Gen Z Pioneer. I do not doubt that there are some generational overlays, and I am not advancing the case that Operators of all ages are identical in their motivations and behaviors at work. A good example of the importance of archetypes is visible in the impact of a firm's mission and vision.

Older and Younger, Women and Men

We asked how important a company's mission and vision was when making a career decision, for example, to stay with, or to leave, a particular firm. Around 60% of workers said it was important. Half of those (31% of the total) declared it very important. This is encouraging for firms who invest to develop and communicate their missions. In fact, 43% of Gen Z workers said it was very important. But then again, 36% of Millennials said it was very important, too. And so did 22% of workers over 45 years old. (In some countries, India, for example, the Millennials actually care about mission more than Gen Z.)

In fact, archetypes are a better predictor of the importance of mission when making career decisions than age groups. While 70% of Pioneers and 63% of Givers said it was very important, just 41% of Artisans did. Corroboration that mission often means something special to these two archetypes comes from the question we asked about sources of energy at work. Pioneers and Givers called out "the positive impact of my firm's mission/vision" as a far more important energy source for them than for any of the other archetypes. Unless we disaggregate the age groups, we risk making misleading assumptions about their common motivations and needs at work.

The truly remarkable fact about workers who judge mission to be very important is not that they are young. It is that their mission-focus is associated with feeling highly satisfied in their jobs – more than twice as satisfied as workers who care less about the mission – at all age levels and at all stress levels. I noted earlier that in aggregate, the "positive impact of my firm's mission/vision" was the lowest ranked source of energy. When you look differentially at workers who care about mission/vision next to those who do not care, the ones who do care, they care a lot. For them it's practically at the top of the list of the 11 energy sources we asked about.

Women and Men

The global workforce participation rate for women has been stuck just under 60% for the last 30 years. It has increased in wealthy countries, but declined in many faster-growing, lower-income ones, like India and Nigeria. Even in China, where the government's commitment to equality of the sexes has been officially reiterated every year since it was introduced in 1995, the participation rate is declining. The recent policy direction is a rallying cry that women should start a "new trend of family," to help the country confront its aging population and chronically low birth rate. That sounds like a reduced emphasis on women at work.[18]

COVID-19 also disproportionately impacted female workforce participation, particularly for non-college-educated women.[19]

Despite different starting points and cultural contexts, every country has an opportunity to bring more women into the workforce to fill talent gaps and advance women's empowerment. Understanding the differences (and similarities) between women and men at work is important for both those agendas.

In our research, what motivates women and men at work is mostly the same. At the global level, there are two small differences and one large one. Women prioritize good relationships at work a little higher than men. They prioritize good compensation a little higher too: I cannot prove it from the research, but I want to believe this is related to the interminable pay gap history where women have earned less than men for the same work.

By far the most noticeable difference is in flexibility, which is 20% more important to women at work than it is to men (to be clear, it's also important to men, second in their ranking of job attributes). Women continue to bear a much greater burden of care at home and carry a disproportionate share of unpaid work, which increases the value of flexibility.

Flexible work arrangements can keep women in the workforce but often at the cost of wage and career advancement. In the United States, twice as many women as men work part-time. They are more likely to take extended leaves.[20] Even for women who continue to work full-time, many may steer away from "high-intensity" jobs that are perceived as less predictable.

There are many aspects to the story of women at work outside the scope of this book. Conscious and unconscious bias continues to infuse workplace structures and systems. While occupations have become more gender-balanced in the last 30 years, women remain underrepresented in many higher-paying management and technical occupations, especially the digital and engineering jobs in heavy demand today (only a quarter of US computing jobs are held by women and only 13% of engineering jobs).[21,22]

The traditional management career ladder has been especially hard for many women: it has rarely been friendly to flexible work models, extended breaks, and on-/off-ramps as part of the journey. Despite all this, a possible cause for optimism is the rise of a new talent model, where a career passport is as important as a career ladder.

Passports and Ladders

The *career ladder* assumes talent aspires to take the same, sequential (and usually linear) upward steps. It is the metaphor that perfectly captures the old norms concept that we are all, managers and labor alike, marching up the same set of steps in pursuit of the same advances.

The *career passport* appeals to men and women at work today who are looking for many kinds of flexibility in their careers. They need a way to get accredited for prior roles at other firms, capabilities mastered, trainings attended, certifications gained, projects completed, results achieved, detours into their side-hustle businesses, and time off the field supporting partners, caring for parents and children, or pursuing personal interests. The passport is owned by the individual, not the firm. It allows firms to pay the person, not the job, and it's a way to navigate around job grading, one of the more debilitating features of the professional management HR playbook.

Job grading, or job leveling, as routinely practiced in firms of scale, does have a role to play but is the antithesis of the career passport mindset. A growing minority of today's workers – we do not yet know what proportion – prefer to picture their career as a series of what Reid Hoffman, a founder of LinkedIn, has called "tours of duty," a model of firm/individual relationship based on mutual investment but no presumption of career-long loyalty or commitment.[23] The agility that the firm gains from creating high-quality tours of duty is part of the model's appeal. For some individuals, this might be a dream career. They add value to a firm for a defined period, expand their learning, and then move on to something else, no strings attached. For others, this picture of the firm as Linux or Wikipedia will be less appealing. Your archetype will greatly impact your attraction to this way of managing a career.

Passports can help in another important way. Scale insurgents generally have fewer professional managers, so people need alternative career tracks based on specialist expertise. In the old norms for talent, all deep experts eventually got promoted to management, where some flourished and others did not.

In the new norms, we see more firms imitating companies like Cisco, where there are long-established programs for technically expert employees who do not relish managerial responsibility.

This chapter described an approach for firms to think about their older workers. Male and female older workers want interesting work and autonomy and are substantially more likely to be Givers and Artisans. Firms can succeed with this group through redesigning roles with those motivations in mind while respecting their older person strengths without overly romanticizing them.

Women are clear that their highest priority in a job is good compensation, followed by flexibility, interesting work, job security, and good relationships. This varies by age and by country. Women, of course, are not all the same: there is far greater variation among women than between women and men.

We can use the research to understand those variations. Let's start with differences by country. The four countries where men rate flexibility highest are the United Kingdom, the United States, Canada, and Denmark. These are *also* the four countries where women rate flexibility most important, more than 20% higher than the men. In these economies, everyone wants flexibility at work, but women want it more.

Likewise, the four countries where men rate flexibility lowest – Saudi Arabia, Brazil, Nigeria, and India – are also the ones where women rate flexibility the lowest (although still higher than the men). In these economies, flexibility is just not that important compared to other attributes such as job security or good relationships at work, for men and for women. It may not be over-simplifying to conclude that in places where jobs have been harder to get and harder to keep, flexibility at work is a feature that many workers consider a luxury.

The mix of archetypes is strikingly similar for men and women and follows the same trajectory with age, with a lot more Givers and Artisans among the older cohorts, and fewer Pioneers and Strivers. In countries with a high mix of Pioneers (Nigeria and India), it's high for both men and women. In Japan, where the Striver mix is the highest of all, it's high for men and for women. In countries with a high mix of Operators (the United Kingdom, Italy, France, and Australia), it's high for men and for women.

As you saw in Chapter 5, men and women experience broadly similar stress triggers and have broadly similar sources of energy at work. The number-one source for everyone is that feeling of confidence when you know how to do your job well. And on the related question about what firms can offer to support their workers' wellness, men and women concur on the two most important programs: flexible hours when they are needed and a practical leave of absence policy.

■ ■ ■

De-averaging the workforce will lead to the design of more distinctively shaped career paths, more types of compensation package, and more experiences to be logged in the passport, but will still leave the ladder in place for those who prefer its predictable linearity. Some of these different paths and choices will be based on age, and some on gender. Nonetheless, the data is clear that some age cohorts and some gender cohorts want the same things from work.

We can move on from the convenient but wrong idea that all younger workers have the same motivations, or all older workers or all female workers or all male workers. They do not.

Yes, there are important patterns of behavior that reflect commonalities across these "visible" segments. But it is at the level of the invisible segments – the archetypes – that the deepest differences emerge. Once we understand those, we can redesign talent programs in much more targeted ways.

The Archetype Effect

Chapter 7

Good Jobs

As the second half of the twentieth century unfolded after World War II, with strengthening labor movements, rising real wages, and the growth of a professional management career path, millions of good jobs were created. The features of a good job varied quite a bit by region, with economic conditions, cultural values, and social policies providing distinctive context.

In the United States, unionized jobs in manufacturing and industry with strong benefits, job security, and fair pay created opportunities for home ownership and upward mobility. In the reconstruction of Western Europe, a good job was often linked with strong social safety nets, generous welfare benefits, pensions, and extensive labor protections. In Japan, a good job implied lifetime employment with a focus on loyalty to the company, generous benefits, and seniority-based promotions. In the state-controlled economies of the former Soviet Union and Eastern bloc countries, jobs that contributed to state goals, guaranteed employment, and ensured state-provided benefits such as housing and healthcare were the most valued (with the best jobs being within the party or state apparatus). In a range of developing markets, stability and a reliable income were most critical, often best found in government jobs or growing industries like textiles, mining, and agriculture; urban jobs were preferred over rural ones for the better infrastructure and opportunities.

Over the same period, automation had a significant impact, reducing human involvement in a wide variety of "bad jobs," by taking over tasks that were repetitive, dangerous, required little skill, and were low paid.

Have We Hit Peak Good Jobs?

The firm of the future will have fewer jobs for humans than the firm of the past, all other things equal. Current thinking, nothing more than educated guess-estimation at this stage, suggests that the labor time savings from generative artificial intelligence (GenAI) might be in the range of 20% in the near to medium term (some people, as we have seen, think it will be 100% eventually). Time savings are only one part of the impact. There will be entirely new products and businesses created using GenAI tools. Sooner, perhaps in one to three years, there will be changes to the way people do their current work thanks to GenAI's ability to produce output faster (e.g. call center chat bots), with higher quality (e.g. marketing content creation), and/or at lower cost (e.g. internal knowledge management). Setting aside once again the Musk view that no one will need to work, it is hard to avoid the question – has the share of good jobs peaked?

The answer depends on the definitions. The old norm definition looks a lot like the one I used in preceding paragraphs about the second half of the twentieth century. Those definitions were about the job and took very little account of the person in the job. The new norm definition assumes a good job is part made from the job itself (activities, expected results) and part made from the person holding it. The same exact job might be a great job for a Pioneer but at best only an okay job for an Operator.

As I described in the introduction, the underlying old norm assumptions were that everyone was on the ladder, trying to improve themselves to look more like the most senior people in the firm, that everyone resembled some version of a Striver. In the new norms, those assumptions do not stand up to the reality of diverse human motivations. The most important use for archetypes, through de-averaging workers, is to allow us to humanize jobs and thereby increase the mix of good ones.

The Mystery Once More

The Gen Z marketer in the cubicle next to yours may have more in common with you than you might initially expect (what stresses her out at work, perhaps, what she gets energy from, and what she looks for in a job). Firms have a good sense for these commonalities and have built standardized, at least partly automated, talent management systems around them.

At the same time, that young marketer may be completely different from you at the core of her motivation. She dislikes the repetitiveness of the monthly reviews of return on investment of her marketing spend decisions. She has been in the role for two years. It has not delivered on her learning and growth goals, and even though there is a promotion (her first) on the horizon six months away, she is already looking around for another job. At this stage of her life, like approximately 15% of Gen Z workers around the world, she is an Explorer. She is very willing to trade status and security for the opportunity to learn something new, to have a new work experience.

This seems completely crazy to you. You have patiently plotted your path into a senior marketing role, have earned multiple promotions from your dogged hard work, have celebrated each new job title, and even though you are barely mid-career, switching firms now is not part of the plan. You, like 21% of the world's workers, are a Striver.

When the young marketer leaves, there is a good chance the exit interview will be a terrible experience for both of you. You are frustrated and find it hard to understand why she is quitting even before she has a new job lined up; she will feel your messages about "staying the course" and "toughing it out" completely miss what she is looking for at work. Afterward, you may shake your head and blame it on her being a Gen Z with a short attention span and no ability to make sacrifices for career progress.

In fact, she *will* make sacrifices for the things she cares most about. She is just being who she is at work: an Explorer.

If this young marketer were not an employee but a customer (which of course she is, at different times of the week), the firm would use conjoint and other discrete choice analytics to understand the trade-offs she is making between stability and new experiences, between status and freedom, and between compensation and variety. It would understand in detail the trigger points for her decisions. It would model out the value of creating a product that meets her combination of needs relative to her willingness to pay for it. It would decide if she is a "must win" or one of group of customers it is willing to alienate or lose to make space for better ones. The mystery is why firms know so few of the answers to these questions about their workers.

Confident Archetypes, Fearful Archetypes

"What really energizes me is hitting my sales goals and being recognized in front of my peers," says 45-year-old Pedro, a sales manager from Brazil, who is a Striver.

"My free time is the most important thing to me. My mantra is work smarter, not harder," says 23-year-old Adam, a youth campaigns coordinator from the United States, who is an Operator.

People weigh different job attributes differently, as we have seen time and time again in the research. We have also learned from cognitive science and behavioral economics over the last 20 years that our judgments are subject to many types of bias and that we use different models for decision-making, especially under uncertainty.

For example, there is uncertainty when people are considering a job change. Operators might be sensitive to loss aversion, fearing the potential risks of changing jobs more than the potential benefits. Artisans may be prone to overconfidence bias, believing so strongly in their unique skills but underestimating the challenge of finding new opportunities that give them the same amount of autonomy. Explorers may be strongly influenced by the framing effect of how a new job is presented to them (for example, responding positively when what is highlighted are new challenges and learning opportunities).

Whether people move jobs and whether they are satisfied or unsatisfied in a job has as much to do with their archetype as with the job itself. If we agree that firms have to play the twin roles of creating good "stuff" (whatever their stuff may be) and creating good jobs, then we should want to get as much insight as possible about what motivates workers into the hands of people designing jobs.

Workers are motivated differently, while sharing some common aspirations, and they are stressed by different triggers, with some common themes. Workload and long hours share the gold medal for inducing stress, across countries, age groups, and archetypes. On average, stress makes people less satisfied at work, although we cannot ignore the sizable minority of all workers (and the very sizable mix of executives) who are able to combine being highly stressed with being highly satisfied. Stress tolerance, in other words, is not evenly distributed (this would be very clear if we did the conjoint or trade-off analysis I referenced earlier).

Coming to the rescue of stressed-out workers is a set of potential energy sources, which we can assert are all aspects of a good job. Doing work you are interested in; seeing results from the work you do; feeling job secure; feeling safe; and above all, feeling confident that you have the ability to do your job well.

With those energy creators in place, the "Confident Archetype" can come to work every day. Operators enjoy the command they feel of predictable work routines and the camaraderie of their colleague-friends. Givers know that they definitely improved the lives of others that day. Artisans see the value of their deep mastery being used in the firm. Explorers are excited to be handed a new assignment. Strivers enjoy approaching the next milestone on the horizon. Pioneers feel enabled to propose another visionary change idea.

A good job is not good because it allows individuals to find their personal meaning and purpose at work; this deus ex machina is not required. For those who do find it, we should celebrate their fulfilment. For most workers, this is not the goal, and least of all for Operators, Strivers and Explorers, who do not typically expect meaning, self-worth, intrinsic purpose, or a sense of personal identity from work.

Every archetype also has a version of itself that is tired, or angry, or feeling lazy: the "Fearful Archetype." Work is a grind, and there is too much of it. Operators are annoyed that their boss refused flex hours on the day of their son's special football game. The usually selfless Givers wake up wondering, What about me? Is there enough in this for me? Artisans have a panic about mandatory retirement, which they in particular dread. Explorers are disillusioned by a career chat where the manager painted a picture of a four-year journey to the next milestone (and on a skill trajectory they have mostly lost interest in). Strivers feel under-recognized. Pioneers are offended at feedback that they are hard to work with.

Good jobs help keep workers in the Confident zone, no matter what motivations they are driven by.

Governments Can Help

Governments have a role to play. As we saw in the Nordic countries, governments can create regulatory frameworks covering workers' rights, minimum wage laws, unemployment benefits, and labor market intermediation. When these complement social values and common worker motivations, positive consequences result.

Governments also look ahead to future skill needs and design programs to plug the gaps between today and a competitive economy in the next generation. Programs are often focused on digital or STEM skills, although it depends on government priorities (for example, Rwanda launched a program specifically aimed at upskilling the population to support tourism, mostly through English language skills).[1] The level of investment differs significantly by country, ranging from a few free online courses to a fully-fledged government body running job festivals, systems of credits for firms and individuals, online tracking portals, and fellowships.

The World Economic Forum (WEF) dreams of a Reskilling Revolution, and in 2020 launched programs in 30 countries whose combined ambition is to provide one billion people with better education, more skills, and increased economic opportunity by 2030.[2]

Singapore's SkillsFuture program is a current standout. More than 20% of working Singaporeans have now taken at least one of the 29,000 courses available, on topics from flower-arranging to software code-writing.[3] There are courses for upskilling, reskilling courses for people wanting to make career transitions, and courses for people working in sectors considered vital to the city's future growth. Singapore's Ministry of Education has constructed an eco-system for delivery, involving other government ministries, the major universities, junior colleges, polytechnics, corporates, trade associations, and chambers of commerce. Singapore uses *microcredentials*, which are certifications of assessed competencies that are complementary to a formal qualification, awarded on completion of standalone courses designed to develop specific skills. Other governments around the world do the same, from Uruguay to Canada and China to New Zealand. Microcredentials are affordable, flexible, and personal. They are useful for non-traditional education providers, and they are tailor-made for people building a career passport.

All governments offering these programs realize that the challenge is to make sure there are real linkages between courses offered and on-the-job reality. The ones that work best are those that give people the opportunity to explore how to apply a new skill in their work, rather than assume they can see the applications themselves.

I find myself having the same discussion with governments as with large corporations: for the most part younger workers do not want to be told exactly what career path they should take. They want help to discover their own path. It is powerful for a government to lay out the broad directions they intend for the economy. After that, their highest impact should be to help individuals on their own journeys of discovery, journeys inevitably influenced by archetype.

To Flexibility and Beyond

The chief people officer (CPO) at a multinational, on a mission to improve productivity, satisfaction, and retention, recently decided that the solution was to inject flexibility into every aspect of the HR systems and policies.

This is a good idea. Firms across the world have been building more flexible elements into jobs over the last several decades. There are many ways in which flexibility is highly valuable at work. Here are three, ones we considered in earlier chapters, that influenced the CPO, together with some observations about the limitations of flexibility.

Women workers place a high value on flexibility (quite a bit higher than men, almost everywhere). In fact, flexibility is the single most important job attribute for women in two countries (Australia and the United Kingdom). *However*, everywhere else it is much less important than good compensation, and often behind interesting work and good relationships too. In Saudi Arabia, United Arab Emirates, Brazil, India, and Nigeria (that's about 1.9 billion people in total, with about 650 million of them working), flexibility just barely makes it to fourth position on the list of priorities.

Flexibility is important to older workers. For them, it often shows up in a desire to control their time, perhaps by going freelance or working part-time, on their way to eventual full retirement. Structuring work options against this desire is one thing firms can consider in the already-here or arriving-soon struggle to attract and keep older workers. *However*, flexibility is far less important to most older workers than interesting work and good compensation.

When we asked workers what firms could do to support their wellness at work, the number-one answer was flexible hours when needed. *However*, for some workers, the ability to spend part of their time on "passion projects" was almost as important to their wellness. For others, it was the option to try a fast-track promotion path.

Flexibility is a powerful way to describe the outcome of de-averaging. People management is the next battleground for the integration of scale and intimacy. For intimacy, policies and systems need to be flexible. But the value and specific definition of flexibility vary a lot from one worker to another. For some, it's not even that important: a mid-career Millennial Striver, for example, is not thinking about flexibility very much. There are 1.8 billion Millennials in the world, approximately two-thirds of them working; 20% of them are Strivers, and for those roughly 250M workers, flexibility at work is a nice to have, but far from critical to productivity or satisfaction.

A narrow view of flexibility, centered on flexible hours and remote work policies, is still a good idea, but on its own, not nearly enough. Because there is no such thing as an average worker, the flexibility we need in talent systems goes deeper, all the way to shaping assignments, career paths, compensation and evaluation systems, time-off policies, around distinct sets of motivation.

A new generation of digital, AI-assisted human resource management tools will reduce the cost of administering jobs that already exist. They may also improve our ability to match ourselves to jobs. If we feed the models multiple aspects of who we are at work: skills, achievements, qualifications, prior roles, current roles, trainings, motivations – all the pages in our passport – then in return they will feed us insights into our current performance and potential pathways.

The models will also feed our organizations information that improves their ability to collaborate with us on the design of a career journey. At least for those who want a journey. The model can also help us appreciate an Operator like Beverley, and the hundreds of millions like her, for whom a job is just a job. It can help to design roles that allow her to bring her best self to work just as much as for the Explorer who wants a transfer to another division, for the Striver with their eyes set on a leadership role, or for the Pioneer, working nights and weekends on a start-up plan that's going to change the world.

Solving the Mystery

Approximately 3.5 billion people went to work today (a little more than 2 billion men, a little under 1.5 billion women). Two billion of them say they are *struggling* at work. 1.4 billion were *stressed* out for much of the day. More than 500 million are *actively disengaged* from their work. Almost 1.2 billion are simply *not engaged*.[4]

Is this the best we can do? What is the gap between the experience of these workers and the 1.2 billion who are *thriving* or the 500 million *actively engaged*?

The mystery is why organizations know so little about their workers' motivations. They can start with the simplest of questions: Why do you go to work? Who are you when you get there?

The answers are, of course, it depends. Archetypes open the door into a real discussion about how it depends. Nothing too fussy. No cradle-to-grave, you are-either-one-thing-or-its-opposite behavioral straitjacket. A simple, practical, yet rigorously data-driven way for us to understand ourselves at work, to appreciate how others are the same and different from us, to build high-functioning teams using that awareness, and to help leaders design good jobs for the richly diverse workers at their firm. That's the *Archetype Effect,* and it's available to everyone, now.

Epilogue

After about a year into her product manager role at the payments firm, Jing met a colleague of mine at a social event, where she opened up about the challenges of her job. The colleague encouraged her to take the archetype quiz, right then and there. She scored very high on Giver, with Striver next highest, a little below.

Jing was interested in this outcome and slightly bothered by it. She asked if she could take the full research survey, the same one we used on close to 50,000 global workers. She studied those results like the well-trained analyst that she is. She was aware that she still felt competitive at work sometimes and got a lot from the promotions and recognitions that had been part of her life since primary school. But the full research fleshed out the quiz's conclusion that Jing brings many of the Giver's values and priorities to work. She cares about her own learning and growth. It is important to her to make a decent income although she has never felt especially motivated by money, even when she was earning well for her age at Alibaba. Mostly, though, she thrives when she is building deep personal relationships, helping to create team spirit, and feeling like she is helping her colleagues do well. She thought back to her time at Alibaba getting the new analysts settled in, and specifically the few months she had spent planning the customer conference.

She remembered the way her mother had described what she loved about being a school teacher.

The cross-functional product teams she managed at the new firm were frequently arguing. The founders had consciously created a culture where conflict and disagreement were welcomed, in the name of the best product and customer experience. There also wasn't a lot of time to think about the experience that team members were having: they were always up against intense deadlines. But she had survived working at Alibaba for almost four years. That was no small achievement. Besides, Jing's parents had instilled in her the idea that work was supposed to be hard and that doing whatever it took to get the job done was normal. She now had language for this aspect of herself at work: she was in large part a Striver.

The thought she carried around in her head every day was that she was also a Giver, maybe even to a greater degree. She now had a way to understand why she had taken on so many of the young hires at the payments firm as mentees and why she had volunteered to organize the summer company event. It was not that she wanted more work. It was feeding a deeper need that she had not been conscious of before. Even though she enjoyed the mentoring and the event organization, she was feeling frustrated and a touch resentful that she received essentially no recognition from her bosses for these other contributions. It was as if the firm hardly valued her doing them at all.

She started to ask others to take the archetype quiz and was not surprised to learn that on her product teams she was surrounded by Pioneers, Explorers, and Artisans. Jing is becoming a good manager, and she's always been a quick learner. Almost immediately, she was able to make some adjustments to the way she managed the team that took more account of the different motivations of its members – particularly for one

Artisan, whom she had mistakenly assumed was a difficult and arrogant engineer, when in fact all he wanted was to be left alone to write code.

She approached her friend in People Operations and shared her worker archetype with him. A few weeks later he invited her to join a project team that was tasked with redesigning the performance management programs. This was overdue. There were now more than 700 people at the firm, in three different locations, and everyone seemed to have a different understanding of their career path, their compensation plan, and how they were performing.

There is no fairy tale ending here. Jing has not woken up one day to find her ultra-Pioneer founder bosses suddenly converted to a 9-to-5, predictable working style with no overtime and lots of public praise for their colleagues. She is still a product manager. The teams still argue. She still enjoys multiple parts of her role. What's new is that she has started to understand who she is at work and what she finds most motivating. This knowledge is leading her to consider some career directions that look different than the ones she assumed for herself as a fresh graduate.

Getting fired for no real reason changed something in Jing. No one ever tells a Striver to strop striving, but a chance encounter at a social event has caused her to question whether she really wants the perpetual hustle.

She does not know her exact path forward yet. For now, she's a Giver and a Striver, and for now she's trying to be responsive to both sets of motivations, even if they sometimes conflict. She received a pay increase at the end of her first year. Her product teams are on track. The performance management redesign is progressing well. Her parents are delighted.

167

Epilogue

Notes

Introduction

1. Bloomberg (2023). More Than One-Third of American Workers Turn to Freelance Jobs in 2023. http://www.bloomberg.com/news/articles/2023-12-12/record-64-million-americans-turn-to-gig-work-in-2023-survey (accessed 7 August 2024).
2. HR One (2023). The Rise of Gig Workers: Navigating Legal and HR Implications in China. http://www.hrone.com/blog/the-rise-of-gig-workers (accessed 7 August 2024).
3. Ipso (2021). Workers Want More Flexibility from Their Employers After COVID. http://www.ipsos.com/en-us/news-polls/return-to-the-workplace-global-survey (accessed 7 August 2024).
4. Porter, M. E. (1985). *Competitive Advantage: Creating and Sustaining Superior Performance.* New York: Free Press.
5. Jiang, Z. and Gong, X. (2019). The research on human resource development of tencent—The HR three pillar model. *Journal of Human Resource and Sustainability Studies*, 7, 462-474. doi: 10.4236/jhrss.2019.73030.
6. Shopify UX (2020). What Do You Want to Be When You Grow Up? http://ux.shopify.com/what-do-you-want-to-be-when-you-grow-up-15a0590e2c3a (accessed 7 August 2024).
7. Business Insider (2024). Nvidia Boss Believes CEO Should Have the Most Direct Reports. http://www.businessinsider.com/nvidia-jensen-huang-ceo-should-have-most-direct-reports-2024-3 (accessed 7 August 2024).
8. Chen, C. (2022). *Work Pray Code: When Work Becomes Religion in Silicon Valley.* New Jersey: Princeton University Press.

Chapter 1

1. Keynes, J. M. (1930). Economic Possibilities for Our Grandchildren. http://www.econ.yale.edu/smith/econ116a/keynes1.pdf (accessed 9 August 2024).
2. Smithsonian Magazine (2017). Mail Delivery by Rocket Never Took Off. http://www.smithsonianmag.com/smart-news/mail-delivery-rocket-never-took-180963557 (accessed 9 August 2024).
3. CNN Business (2020). Nanobots, Ape Chauffeurs and Flights to Pluto: The Predictions for 2020 We Got Horribly Wrong. http://www.cnn.com/2020/01/01/tech/2020-predictions-we-got-wrong-scli-intl/index.html (accessed 9 August 2024).
4. Gershuny, J. (2022). Mass media, leisure, and home IT: A panel time-diary approach. *IT & Society*, vol. 1, no. 1, pp. 53–66.
5. ILO. Statistics on Working Time. http://www.ilostat.ilo.org/topics/working-time (accessed 9 August 2024).
6. *HR Magazine* (2023). AI Will End All Jobs, Elon Musk Says. http://www.hrmagazine.co.uk/content/news/ai-will-end-all-jobs-elon-musk-says (accessed 9 August 2024).
7. General Motors Personnel Staff (1961). *The Secret of Getting Ahead*. Montclair, New Jersey: *The Economics Press Inc.*
8. Ibid, pp. 2–3.
9. *HBS Working Knowledge* (2005). The Truck Driver Who Reinvented Shipping. http://hbswk.hbs.edu/item/the-truck-driver-who-reinvented-shipping (accessed 9 August 2024).
10. *Wall Street Journal* (2024). GE Sells Crotonville, a Training Ground for Generations of Managers. http://www.wsj.com/real-estate/commercial/ge-sells-crotonville-campus-13fd35a0 (accessed 9 August 2024).
11. Sloan, A. P. (1963). *My Years with General Motors*. New York City: Crown Publishing Group.
12. Taylor, F. W. (1911). *The Principles of Scientific Management*. Mineola, NY: Dover Publications.
13. Ibid, p. 3.
14. Ibid, p. 3.

15. Ibid, p. 20.

16. Ibid, p. 74.

17. Amazon (2021). 2020 Letter to Shareholders. http://www.aboutamazon .com/news/company-news/20020-letter-to-shareholders (accessed 9 August 2024).

18. Roethlisberger, F. J. and Dickson, W. J. (1939). *Management and the Worker: An Account of a Research Program Conducted by the Western Electric Company.* Chicago: Hawthorne Works

19. Levitt, S. D., and List, J. A. (2011). Was there really a Hawthorne effect at the Hawthorne plant? An analysis of the original illumination experiments. *American Economic Journal: Applied Economics*, vol. 3, no. 1, pp. 224–38.

20. Drucker, Peter. *Concept of the Corporation.* 1946.

21. Ibid, p. 140.

22. Drucker, P. (1978). *Adventures of a Bystander.* London: Routledge.

23. Drucker, P. (1967). *The Effective Executive: The Definitive Guide to Getting the Right Things Done.* New York: Harper.

24. Ferrarie, K. (2005). Processes to assess leadership potential keep Shell's talent pipeline full. *Journal of Organizational Excellence.* www .onlinelibrary.wiley.com/doi/abs/10.1002/joe.20059 (accessed 9 August 2024).

25. YouTube (2015). Zappos CEO Tony Hsieh explains holacracy and why it works for Zappos. http://www.youtube.com/watch?v=-mdlnmJqpHg (accessed 9 August 2024).

26. Harvard Business Review (1994). Revolution at Oticon A/S: The Spaghetti Organization. http://www.store.hbr.org/product/revolution-at-oticon-a-s-the-spaghetti-organization-condensed/IMD083 (accessed 9 August 2024).

27. Valve (2012). Valve: Handbook for New Employees. https://steamcdn-a .akamaihd.net/apps/valve/Valve_NewEmployeeHandbook.pdf (accessed 9 August 2024).

28. Spotify (2014). Spotify Engineering Culture. http://www.engineering .atspotify.com/2014/03/spotify-engineering-culture-part-1 (accessed 9 August 2024).

29. Wall Street Journal (2024). One CEO's Radical Fix for Corporate Troubles. https://www.wsj.com/business/bayer-cuts-bosses-recovery-plan-f3c94865 (accessed 9 August 2024).

Chapter 2

1. Patagonia (2022). Patagonia's Next Chapter: Earth Is Now Our Only Shareholder. http://www.patagoniaworks.com/press/2022/9/14/patagonias-next-chapter-earth-is-now-our-only-shareholder (accessed 12 August 2024).
2. Emre, M. (2019). *What's Your Type?* William Collins.
3. Stein, R. and Swan, A. B. (2019). Evaluating the validity of Myers-Briggs type indicator theory: A teaching tool and window into intuitive psychology. *Soc. Personal. Psychol. Compass.* e12434. https://doi.org/10.1111/spc3.12434
4. Ibid, p. 4.
5. Ibid, p. 7.

Chapter 3

1. Gallup (2024). World Happiness Report 2024. http://www.happiness-report.s3.amazonaws.com/2024/WHR+24.pdf (accessed 14 August 2024).
2. Marketplace (2019). Finland's Flexible Work Blueprint. http://www.marketplace.org/2019/08/14/finland-working-hours-act (accessed 14 August 2024).
3. Justworks (2023). Average PTO Days by Country: How the US Stacks up. https://www.justworks.com/blog/average-vacation-days-by-country#what-countries-have-the-most-vacation-days- (accessed 14 August 2024).
4. Ministry of Foreign Affairs of Denmark (n.d.). The Danish Labour Market. http://www.denmark.dk/society-and-business/the-danish-labour-market (accessed 14 August 2024).

Chapter 4

1. Sloan, A. P. (1963). *My Years with General Motors*. New York: Crown Publishing Group.

2. Ibid, p. 31.
3. Ibid, p. 53.
4. Ibid, p. 58.
5. Ibid, p. 163.
6. Origo, I. (1957). *The Merchant of Prato*. Boston: Godine.
7. Isaacson, W.W. (2011). *Steve Jobs*, p. xxi, New York: Simon & Schuster.
8. Allen, J. (2019). The Bain Micro-Battles System. http://www.bain.com/insights/the-bain-micro-battles-system (accessed 14 August 2024).

Chapter 5

1. Bain (2021). Bain US COVID-19 Consumer/Shopper Survey. https://www.bain.com/insights/shaping-the-consumer-of-the-future/ (accessed 16 August 2024).
2. Chen, C. (2022). *Work Pray Code: When Work Becomes Religion in Silicon Valley*. New Jersey: Princeton University Press.
3. Gallup (2024). State of the Global Workplace: 2024 Report. http://www.gallup.com/workplace/349484/state-of-the-global-workplace.aspx (accessed 16 August 2024).
4. Keynes, J. M. (1930). Economic Possibilities for Our Grandchildren. http://www.econ.yale.edu/smith/econ116a/keynes1.pdf (accessed 16 August 2024).
5. Forbes (2020). 60 Employees Leave Coinbase Over CEO's Pledge to Be Apolitical. http://www.forbes.com/sites/rachelsandler/2020/10/08/60-employees-leave-coinbase-over-ceos-pledge-to-be-apolitical/?sh=3cd994c25a06 (accessed 16 August 2024).
6. Forbes (2020). 60 Employees Leave Coinbase Over CEO's Pledge to Be Apolitical. http://www.forbes.com/sites/rachelsandler/2020/10/08/60-employees-leave-coinbase-over-ceos-pledge-to-be-apolitical/?sh=3cd994c25a06 (accessed 16 August 2024).
7. Friend, J. (2021). Changes at Basecamp. https://world.hey.com/jason/changes-at-basecamp-7f32afc5 (accessed 16 August 2024).
8. The Atlantic (2018). The Murders That Sparked China's Rideshare Boycott. https://www.theatlantic.com/technology/archive/2018/08/didi-murder/568660/ (accessed 16 August 2024).

9. Gallup (2024). State of the Global Workplace: 2024 Report. http://www.gallup.com/workplace/349484/state-of-the-global-workplace.aspx (accessed 16 August 2024).

Chapter 6

1. World Bank (n.d.). World Bank Data on Fertility Rates by Country. www.genderdata.worldbank.org/en/indicator/sp-dyn-tfrt-in (accessed 17 August 2024).
2. Age UK (n.d.). Changes to State Pension Age. www.ageuk.org.uk/information-advice/money-legal/pensions/state-pension/changes-to-state-pension-age (accessed 17 August 2024).
3. NPR (2023). Despite Fierce Protests, France Has Raised the Retirement Age from 62 to 64. http://www.npr.org/2023/04/15/1170246219/despite-fierce-protests-france-has-raised-the-retirement-age-from-62-to-64 (accessed 17 August 2024).
4. Japan Times (2020). Japan to Amend Laws to Help Elderly Work Until 70. www.japantimes.co.jp/news/2020/02/04/national/japan-amend-laws-elderly-work-until-70 (accessed 17 August 2024).
5. SHRM (2024). Singapore's Retirement Age to Be Raised. http://www.shrm.org/topics-tools/employment-law-compliance/singapore-raised-retirement-age (accessed 17 August 2024).
6. Gallup (2018). Snapshot: Average American Predicts Retirement Age of 66. https://news.gallup.com/poll/234302/snapshot-americans-project-average-retirement-age.aspx (accessed 17 August 2024).
7. AARP (n.d.). AARP Global Employer Survey 2020. https://www.aarpinternational.org/file%20library/future%20of%20work/2020-global-employer-survey-annotated-questionnaire.doi.10.26419-2fres.00399.003.pdf (accessed 17 August 2024).
8. Forbes (2024). CEOs Get Serious About Longevity Leadership—in France. http://www.forbes.com/sites/avivahwittenbergcox/2024/02/01/ceos-get-serious-about-longevity-leadership--in-france (accessed 17 August 2024).

9. OECD (n.d.) Promoting an Age-Inclusive Workforce: Living, Learning and Earning Longer. www.oecd-ilibrary.org/sites/15f92878-en/index .html?itemId=/content/component/15f92878-en (accessed 17 August 2024).

10. SHRM (2023). New SHRM Research Details Age Discrimination in the Workplace. http://www.shrm.org/about/press-room/new-shrm-research-details-age-discrimination-workplace (accessed 17 August 2024).

11. Seattle Times (2004). Home Depot, AARP Form Partnership. https:// archive.seattletimes.com/archive/?date=20040613&slug=jmhomede pot13 (accessed 17 August 2024).

12. Washington Post (2013). In Era of Workplace Ageism, Older Workers at NIH Feel Embraced. https://www.washingtonpost.com/local/in-era-of-workplace-ageism-older-workers-at-nih-feel-embraced/2013/11/ 09/b369bb90-4355-11e3-a624-41d661b0bb78_story.html (accessed 17 August 2024).

13. AARP (2021). Employer spotlight: Atos. https://www.aarp.org/work/ employers/employer-spotlight-atos/ (accessed 17 August 2024).

14. OATS (2022). Google.org Makes $10 Million Grant to AARP Foundation to Provide Digital Skills Training. https://oats.org/google-org-makes-10-million-grant-to-aarp-foundation-to-provide-digital-skills-training/ (accessed 17 August 2024).

15. Harvard Business Review (2009). How BMW Is Planning for an Aging Workforce. https://hbr.org/2009/03/bmw-and-the-older-worker (accessed 17 August 2024).

16. Harvard Business Review (2014). Four ways to adapt to an aging workforce. https://hbr.org/2014/04/four-ways-to-adapt-to-an-aging-workforce (accessed 17 August 2024).

17. Allianz (n.d.). Age Inclusion. https://www.allianz.com/en/about-us/ strategy-values/diversity/age-inclusion.html (accessed 17 August 2024).

18. Reuters (2023). A New Trend of Family. https://www.reuters.com/ world/china/xi-says-chinas-women-must-start-new-trend-family-2023-10-30/ (accessed 17 August 2024).

175

19. Pearson Institute for International Economics (2020). COVID-19 widens gender gap in labor force participation in some but not other advanced economies. https://www.piie.com/blogs/realtime-economics/covid-19-widens-gender-gap-labor-force-participation-some-not-other (accessed 17 August 2024).

20. US Bureau of Labor Statistics (2018). Who chooses part-time and why? https://www.bls.gov/opub/mlr/2018/article/who-chooses-part-time-work-and-why.htm (accessed 17 August 2024).

21. National Center for Women in Technology (2016). Women in Tech: The Facts. https://wpassets.ncwit.org/wp-content/uploads/2021/05/13193304/ncwit_women-in-it_2016-full-report_final-web06012016.pdf (accessed 17 August 2024).

22. Harvard Business Review (2016). Why Do So Many Women Who Study Engineering Leave the Field? https://hbr.org/2016/08/why-do-so-many-women-who-study-engineering-leave-the-field (accessed 17 August 2024).

23. Harvard Business Review (2013). Tours of Duty: The New Employer-Employee Compact. https://hbr.org/2013/06/tours-of-duty-the-new-employer-employee-compact (accessed 17 August 2024).

Chapter 7

1. EF (n.d.). EF upskills tourism industry in Rwanda. https://www.ef.edu/about-us/impact/articles/rwanda (accessed 17 August 2024).

2. WEF (2017). Skill, Re-Skill and Re-Skill Again. How to Keep Up with the Future of Work. http://www.weforum.org/agenda/2017/07/skill-reskill-prepare-for-future-of-work (accessed 17 August 2024).

3. SkillsFuture (2024). More Employers and Mid-Career Workers Taking Up SSG-Supported Training. www.skillsfuture.gov.sg/newsroom/more-employers-and-mid-career-workers-taking-up-ssg-supported-training (accessed 17 August 2024).

4. Gallup (2024). State of the Global Workplace: 2024 Report. http://www.gallup.com/workplace/349484/state-of-the-global-workplace.aspx (accessed 17 August 2024).

Acknowledgments

My deepest thanks to Bain colleagues past and present: Jimmy Allen, Andrew Schwedel, Karen Harris, Tov Mindel, Mike Haslett, Nicole Bitler, Eric Garton, Eric Almquist, John Hazan, Yidi Wang, Neelima Jain, Shreyas Raj Krishna, Dunigan O'Keeffe, Russ Hagey, and Erika Serow.

I am greatly indebted to Ong Chin-Yin, Jumin Wong, Paddy Jordan, Anne-Christine Ahrenkiel, Shirley Ko, Professor Hayagreeva Rao, Avivah Wittenberg-Cox, and Zachary Schisgal for their encouragement and critical inputs.

Special thanks to my family: the younger, the older, and those no longer with us, for the love, support, and all the books.

About the Author

James Root is a Senior Partner at Bain & Company and Chair of Bain Futures.

During his more than 30 years at Bain across Europe, North America, and Asia, he has served as Managing Director of Bain New York; as the leader of the Asia Pacific Organization Practice; and as Chair of Bain's Nominating Committee.

His work has concentrated on corporate transformations involving strategy, organizational change, and operational improvement.

During a leave of absence, he cofounded and served as president of a business process outsourcing firm based in Malaysia, where he was responsible for the company's business operations.

He is a Fellow of Hughes Hall College, Cambridge; an Adjunct Professor on the faculty at Hong Kong University of Science & Technology; and a guest lecturer at the Institute for Business and Finance at Waseda University in Tokyo.

A graduate of Cambridge University and London Business School, Root lives in Hong Kong.

Index

Note: Page references with *f* refer to figures.

General Motors Acceptance
    Corporation (GMAC),
    establishment, 92
Generation Z
    archetype mix, 143
    definition, 142
    images, enlargement, 144
    mystery, 155–156
    Operator, Millennial Operator
        (comparison), 145
    work, COVID-19 (impact), 143
    workers, dissatisfaction, 142
Generative AI (GenAI) tools,
    79–82
    usage, 154
Geographic expansion, 100
Gerwig, Greta, 111
Givers (worker archetype), 34–35,
    47, 59
    Artisans, contrast, 63–64
    camaraderie, 50–51
    compensation consideration, 53
    Explorers, contrast, 64
    high-stress workers, 120
    Operators, alliance, 65
    perspective, 73
    Pioneers, contrast, 61
    Strivers, contrast, 60–61
Glassdoor, 27
Global employer survey, 134–135
Governments, impact, 159–161
Grand Career System (Tokyo Gas),
    139–140
Grandternity, 78
Great Sabbatical, 134
Griffith, Tricia, 42
Group of Seven workers,
    characteristics, 133–134
Growth
    approach, 100
    job attribute, 48–49
    older worker perspective, 140

H
Hands-on leadership, 115
Happiness, job satisfaction
    (contrast), 83–84
Hawthorne effect, 18–20
Hawthorne experiments, 16–20
High-intensity jobs, avoidance, 148
Hoffman, Reid, 149
Holacracy, adoption, 26–27
Hollub, Vicki, 111
Home Depot/AARP partnership, 139
Hopelessness, sense, 144–145
Hsieh, Tony
Huffington, Arianna (career/
    journey), 40
Human resource management,
    changes, 85
Human resource management
    systems (HRMSs), 26
    building, 69
    platforms, improvements, 80–81
Hyatt Roller Bearing Company,
    acquisition, 88–89

I
Industry sector details, importance,
    125
Information, increase, 80–81
Initiative/incentive, ideas (basis), 11
Innovations, support, 25–26
Interesting work (job attribute), 47
    male/female older worker
        attraction, 150
Inter-generational conflict, 134
Internal knowledge management,
    154
Intrinsic purpose, 158
Isaacson, Walter, 103

J
Japan workers, stress/job
    dissatisfaction, 145

185

Index

186

Index

187

Index

189

Index